WILLIAM KENTRIDGE
MUIZENBERG

WARREN SIEBRITS

STEIDL

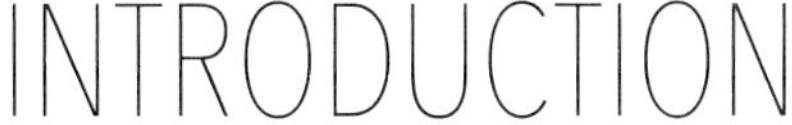

INTRODUCTION

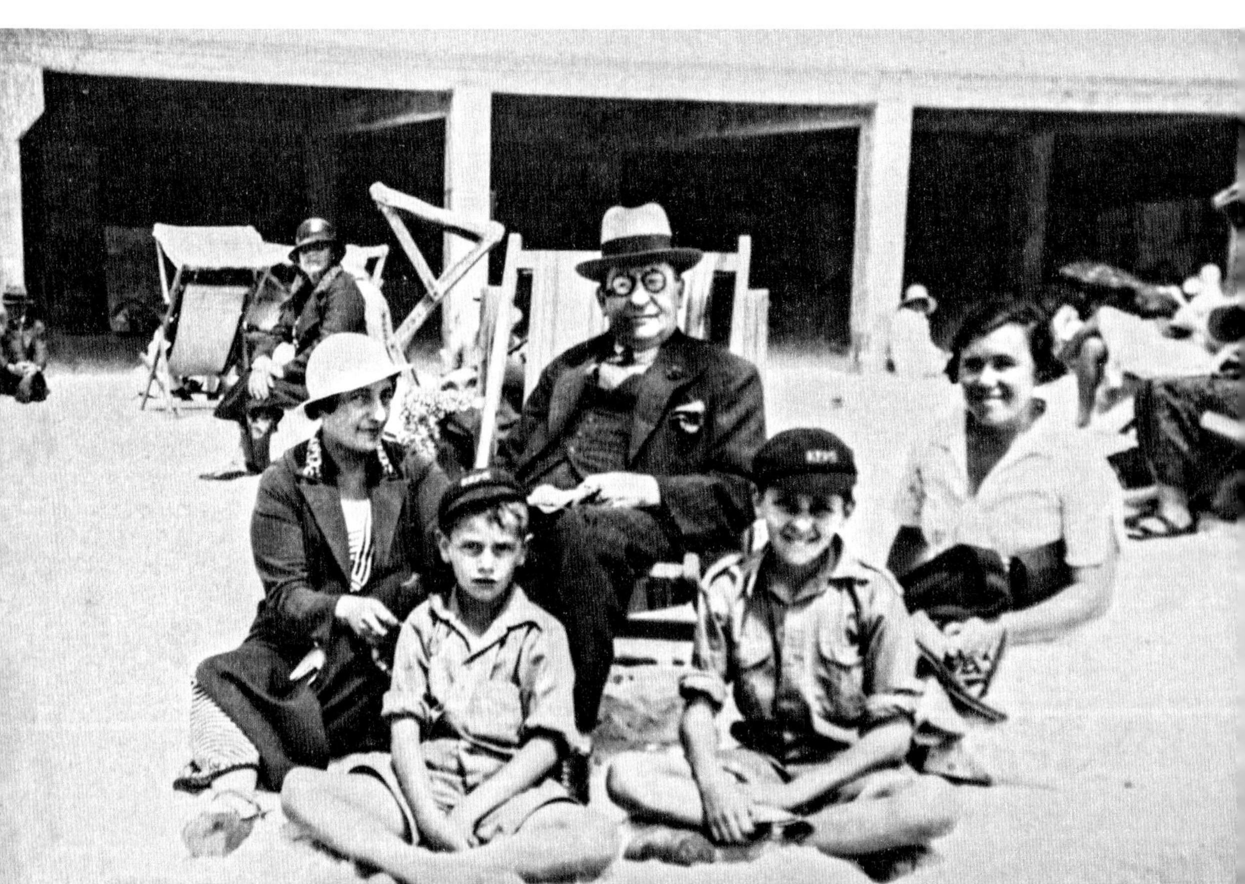

Morris and May Kentridge, their sons Arnold and Sydney, with childminder, Edith Boon on Muizenberg beach, Cape Town, 1934.

Malcolm, Dear,

We'll send a price list so that you can 'get-in' your orders well in advance—laundry bags excluded—wish you could be here too.

Steven

The big painting has at best been finished (almost) after several more transformations + will be stuck up on the exhibition. Also the Muizenberg lino-works + some new etchings + drawings.

Love William

William & Steven are about to make their fortunes. I am earning R1,50 per hour keeping people alive. Pay deducted if I don't.

Love Anne

—Short letter on the back of a Gallery AKIS 101 invitation written by Steven Sack, William Kentridge and Anne Stanwix to Malcolm Purkey in Binghamton, New York, 23 October 1978

My engagement with William Kentridge as an artist has been consistent since I was first exposed to his work in the late eighties. This interest of mine culminated in the opportunity to compile a catalogue raisonné of Kentridge's prints and posters, a project I have been working on since 2019. To date, I have completed the first volume of the catalogue raisonné spanning the years 1974 to 1990 and I am now in the final stages of completing the second volume, which covers the subsequent fourteen years from 1991 to 2004. The first volume of the catalogue raisonné was an opportunity to examine Kentridge's earliest output as a printmaker, including work that had largely been brushed over as 'student work' by those looking critically at Kentridge's oeuvre. The perfunctory engagement with these early but, in my opinion, pivotal images has spurred me on to create a collection of smaller publications with a pointed focus on the aforementioned prints.

The first book in this vein looks at the *Domestic Scenes* (1980) etchings, where Kentridge works and re-works the etching plate in the proofing process, creating multiple state proofs for each print, which recall the drawing and re-drawing technique used in his charcoal animated films. The *Carlton Centre Games Arcade* (1977) etchings are the focus of the second publication. These etchings, which highlighted a Johannesburg landmark and had never been exhibited, were Kentridge's first focused use of etching techniques whilst taking on the role of student and teacher at Ainslie's Studios, Saxonwold, Johannesburg. This third book in the series focuses on a small body of work made between 1976 and 1977, *Muizenberg*. This is the earliest thematically linked series of images produced by Kentridge and—although it includes one etching, *Already Dead Awaiting Stuffing* (Siebrits 16)—the prints are predominantly linocuts.

I have always admired Kentridge's conceptual approach to art making, especially as an artist in South Africa during apartheid. He has a keen observational eye and an uncanny ability to engage with his position—as a privileged white, male South African—with healthy cynicism and an acute awareness of the socio-political landscape. This approach is evident in Kentridge's early print production. With *Domestic Scenes,* Kentridge examines the frivolities of domestic life in apartheid South Africa in the mid-eighties during a very tumultuous time before the National Party government instituted a second state of emergency in 1985. The *Carlton Centre Games Arcade* prints are images capturing the homeless black men living informally in Johannesburg in the hopes of finding employment. With *Muizenberg,* Kentridge creates images of the well-to-do members of South Africa's Jewish community enjoying the summer sun on the 'whites-only' Muizenberg beach. These are the proverbial frogs in the pot, seemingly oblivious to the devastating effects of the apartheid system. As stated by Kentridge in an earlier interview:

1976 was my last year as a student at the University of the Witwatersrand and, as I had majored in political science, the question of alienation, from the early writings of Karl Marx, was very present. I was very aware of the subjects' excess of whiteness, of large people and, particularly, large women. It was a mixture of erotic attraction to that largeness and a sense of it as the over-indulgence of white privilege.

[…]

The political context was a given. I wasn't interrogating the politics and white privilege but it was certainly there in the background, part of the impetus behind the works.

It has been so interesting to discover, in the course of my research, that, instead of there being only a few images relating to the *Muizenberg* series, there are in fact twelve different images and over twenty related impressions if you include all the plate progressions and variations. Kentridge explained to me, in a 2019 interview, that all these prints (bar *Muizenberg 1933* (S.10)) were produced using reference sketches made in situ on Muizenberg Beach over the 1976 December holiday, just after he had completed his final year of university. In the process of trawling through the Kentridge archive, in my effort to finish the second volume of the catalogue raisonné, I was delighted to locate the very sketchbook containing the original reference sketches. These sketches were all done in pencil, as Kentridge was yet to discover his affinity with charcoal, and one can clearly see how elements of each page influenced or were incorporated into the making of the *Muizenberg* prints. It is not often that we have the opportunity to see the full conceptual arc in the creation of an image by an artist. This is what the sketchbook allows and, for this reason, I thought it imperative to reproduce the sketchbook, in full, in this publication.

But the sketchbook does not include any reference to the very first Muizenberg-themed print by Kentridge, *Muizenberg 1933*. This print was made with a very specific family photograph as reference. I had not seen this photograph so I enlisted the aid of Anne Stanwix, Kentridge's wife and consummate Kentridge family archivist, who was able to locate it with ease. Another piece of ephemera that I am happy to reproduce in this publication, the photograph depicts Kentridge's grandfather, Morris Kentridge, seated on a pinstriped deckchair wearing a three-piece suit and Homburg in the middle of the beach. Kentridge's father Sydney and uncle Arnold are seated at his feet, while Morris' wife May Kentridge is on his right and childminder Edith Boon is seated to his left. This photograph was not only the catalyst for the making of this early linocut but has also been a foundational image in his practice, as Kentridge explains in his note referring to the linocut:

In retrospect, this became an iconic image for me over many years and many projects, particularly the film Tide Table *[2003] that shows the character Soho Eckstein in his pinstriped suit sitting in a deckchair on the beach, an image that comes very directly from this old family photograph of my grandfather, Morris Kentridge, in his Homburg and suit on the beach with my father, my uncle and a childminder seated on the sand next to them. Muizenberg was not my childhood holiday place but my father's site. I think there was something about the incongruity of the suit and the beach and the stripe of the deckchair...*

So it is clear that the Muizenberg prints, although very early, are incredibly meaningful to Kentridge and have played an essential role in his conceptual framework over the years. That being said, I must offer a personal anecdote. In 2004, I was in the second year of running my gallery, Warren Siebrits Modern and Contemporary Art, on Jan Smuts Avenue in Rosebank, Johannesburg. At this point, I had been working in the South African art world for fifteen years and was well known to Kentridge. He would frequently visit the gallery to see the exhibitions I had curated, which often included his early prints of which I had always been so fond. One of Kentridge's oldest friends, Timothy James, whom he had met while studying at the University of the Witwatersrand, was looking to sell part of his own Kentridge collection. Kentridge, knowing of my interest in his work and having an appreciation for my approach to art dealing, suggested that James contact me for assistance in this matter.

After some correspondence between the two of us, I travelled to Cape Town to meet with James at his home. Given James' long friendship with Kentridge and Kentridge's propensity towards generosity, I was not surprised by the quality, quantity and vintage of the works James had in his collection. Besides my excitement over these artworks, Timothy James and I quickly bonded over our love of art and history as well as our passion for fine wines. This first meeting would lead to an exhibition titled *11 Rare Etchings and Lithographs by William Kentridge,* which was included in the National Antique and Decorative Arts Faire, held from 21 to 25 July 2004 at the Sandton Convention Centre in Johannesburg. James and I have remained good friends.

Through our friendship, James became aware of my passion for art-historical ephemera and, some years after the exhibition, gifted me a small parcel of postcards, photographs and letters from his friendship with Kentridge. A veritable treasure! Within this parcel was a photograph taken by James in the mid-eighties. It shows William Kentridge seated on a large tractor tyre on Danger Beach, Cape Town. At the time the photograph was taken, Kentridge was in his late twenties. He is captured wearing his decade-appropriate aviator sunglasses with pencil and sketchpad in hand, documenting his surroundings. Although the beach in question is not Muizenberg and the photograph was taken some years after the *Muizenberg* prints were made, this image gives us unique insight into how Kentridge worked during those important early years of his art practice. I could then imagine Kentridge sitting quietly on Muizenberg Beach observing the beachgoers around him, committing their likeness to paper so that he could eventually turn them into the wonderful prints reproduced in this book. This seemingly small gesture on James' behalf fed the fire of my interest in these early prints and it is with the utmost pleasure that I share them with you.

Warren Siebrits, Johannesburg, May 2025

NOTES ON PRINTING AND EDITIONING

All impressions from *Muizenberg* are vintage and were individually printed
and published by William Kentridge from the middle of 1976 to the beginning
of 1977. The series includes eleven linocuts and one etching.

The first print in the series, *Muizenberg 1933* (Siebrits 10), was printed
in 1976 at Kentridge's childhood home, 72 Houghton Drive, Johannesburg.
The second image and the only etching in the series, *Already Dead Awaiting
Stuffing* (S.16), was printed by Kentridge during a summer printing workshop
held by Giuseppe Cattaneo at the School of Arts of the University of the
Witwatersrand in early 1977. The remainder of the prints, all linocuts
(S.17–S.26), were printed at Ainslie's Studios, Saxonwold, Johannesburg,
as part of a printmaking course he attended from 1977 to 1978.

When printing the linocuts, Kentridge used newsprint throughout the
proofing process with a small number of impressions, most often in the final
state, printed on mulberry paper. All impressions of the etching were printed
on Fabriano, as newsprint and mulberry paper are too delicate to go through
the etching press.

Due to the fact that this series of prints was never exhibited, only three
of the twelve images were printed in a formal edition: *Muizenberg Beach—
Man with Sunglasses* (S.19), printed in an edition of four impressions and two
artist proofs; *Before* (S.23), printed in an edition of twenty-five impressions;
and *Chest and Chain, Muizenberg* (S.26), printed in an edition of twenty-five
impressions. None of the other prints were marked or numbered.

Another important aspect of this series of images is the presence
of colour. *Already Dead Awaiting Stuffing* is the first of six colour etchings
printed by Kentridge in his entire oeuvre to date (the other five having
been printed between 1977 and 1979 at Ainslie's Studios with the assistance
of Rosanna Mahoney).

WILLIAM KENTRIDGE DISCUSSES THE MAKING OF *MUIZENBERG*, PLATE BY PLATE

Muizenberg 1933

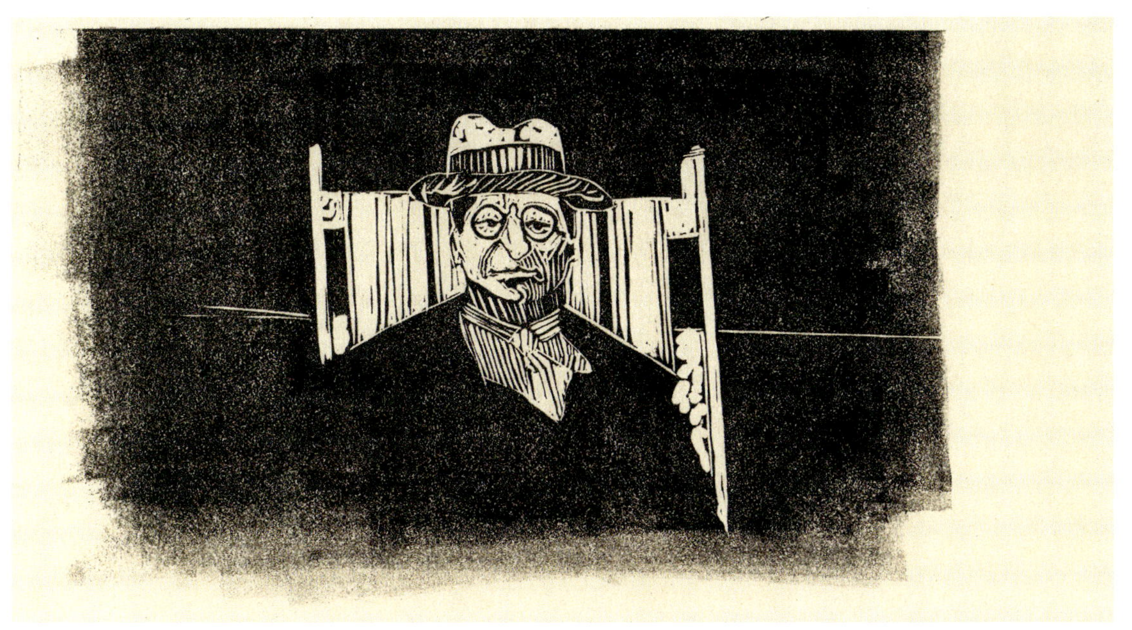

S.10.1 | linocut
image: 15.5 x 25 cm | sheet: 24 x 35.5 cm | paper: newsprint
edition: not editioned, although at least 5 impressions printed; 4 impressions identified at time of publishing
1st state: head without Muizenberg text

Muizenberg 1933

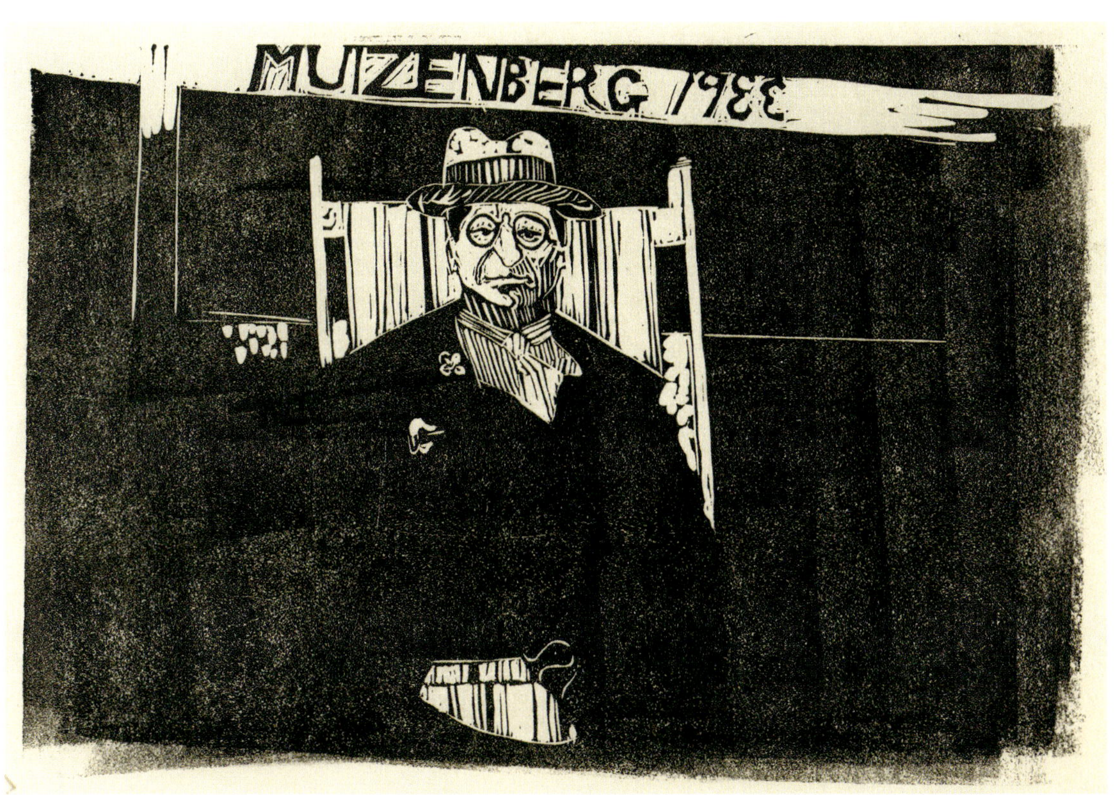

S.10.2 | linocut
image: 21.3 x 31.5 cm | sheet: 23.5 x 35.5 cm | paper: newsprint
edition: not editioned, although at least 5 impressions printed; 4 impressions identified at time of publishing
2nd state: head with Muizenberg text

Muizenberg 1933

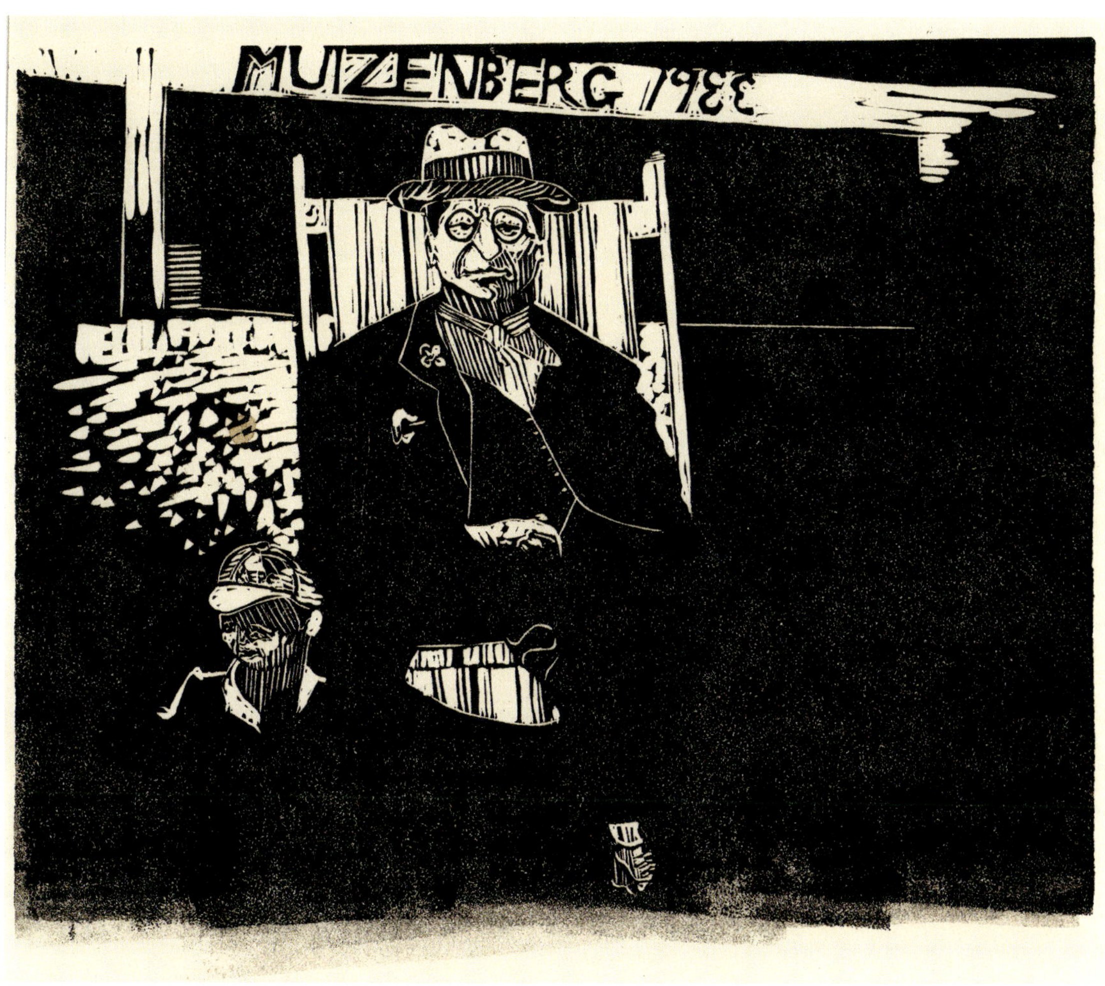

S.10.3 | linocut
image: 26.5 x 33 cm | sheet: 46 x 35.5 cm | paper: newsprint
edition: not editioned, although at least 5 impressions printed; 4 impressions identified at time of publishing
3rd state: Morris and Sydney Kentridge (heads only)

Muizenberg 1933

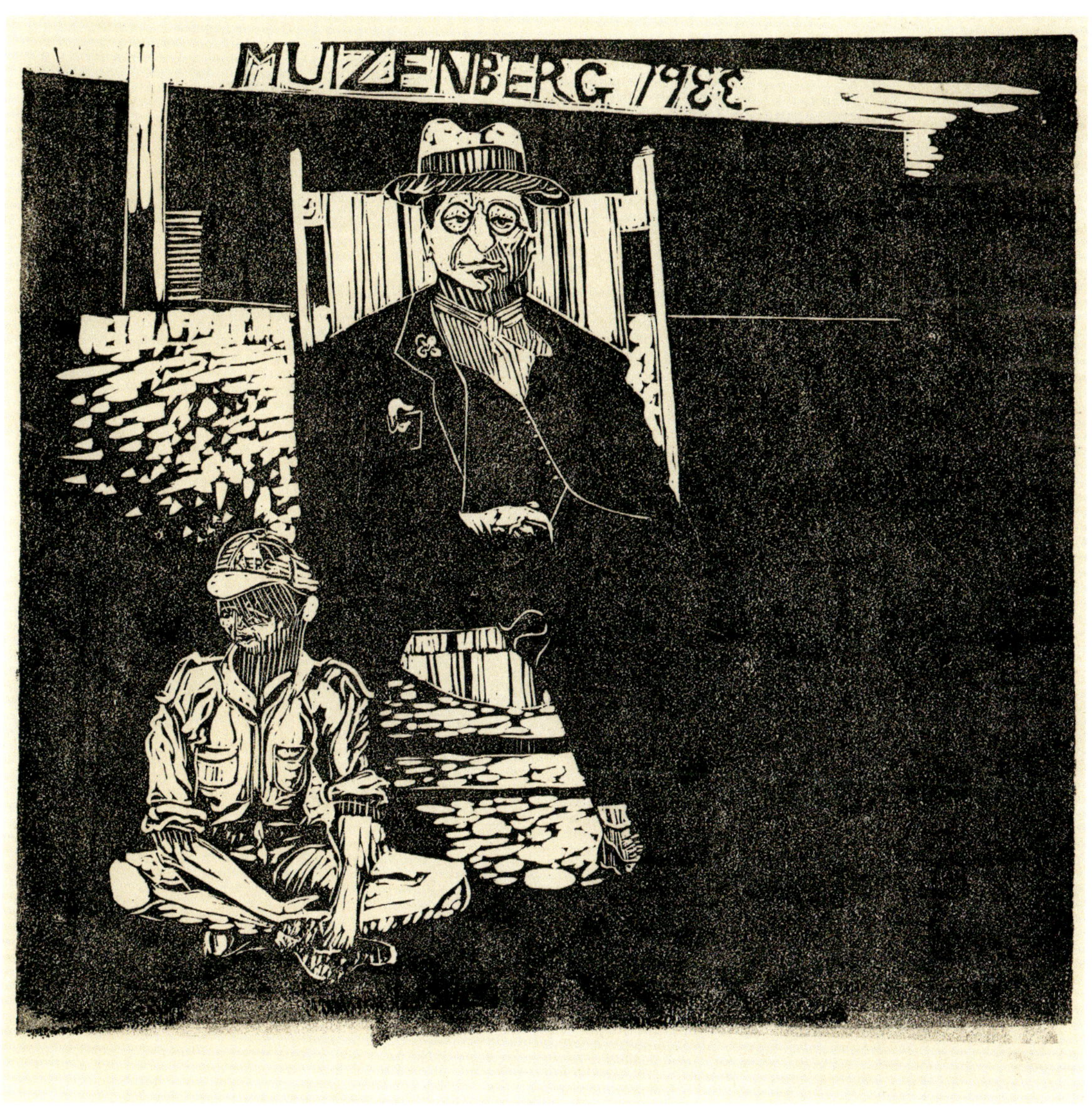

S.10.4 | linocut
image: 30 x 33 cm | sheet: 46.1 x 40.9 cm | paper: newsprint
edition: not editioned, although at least 5 impressions printed; 2 impressions identified at time of publishing
4th state: 2 figures missing

Muizenberg 1933

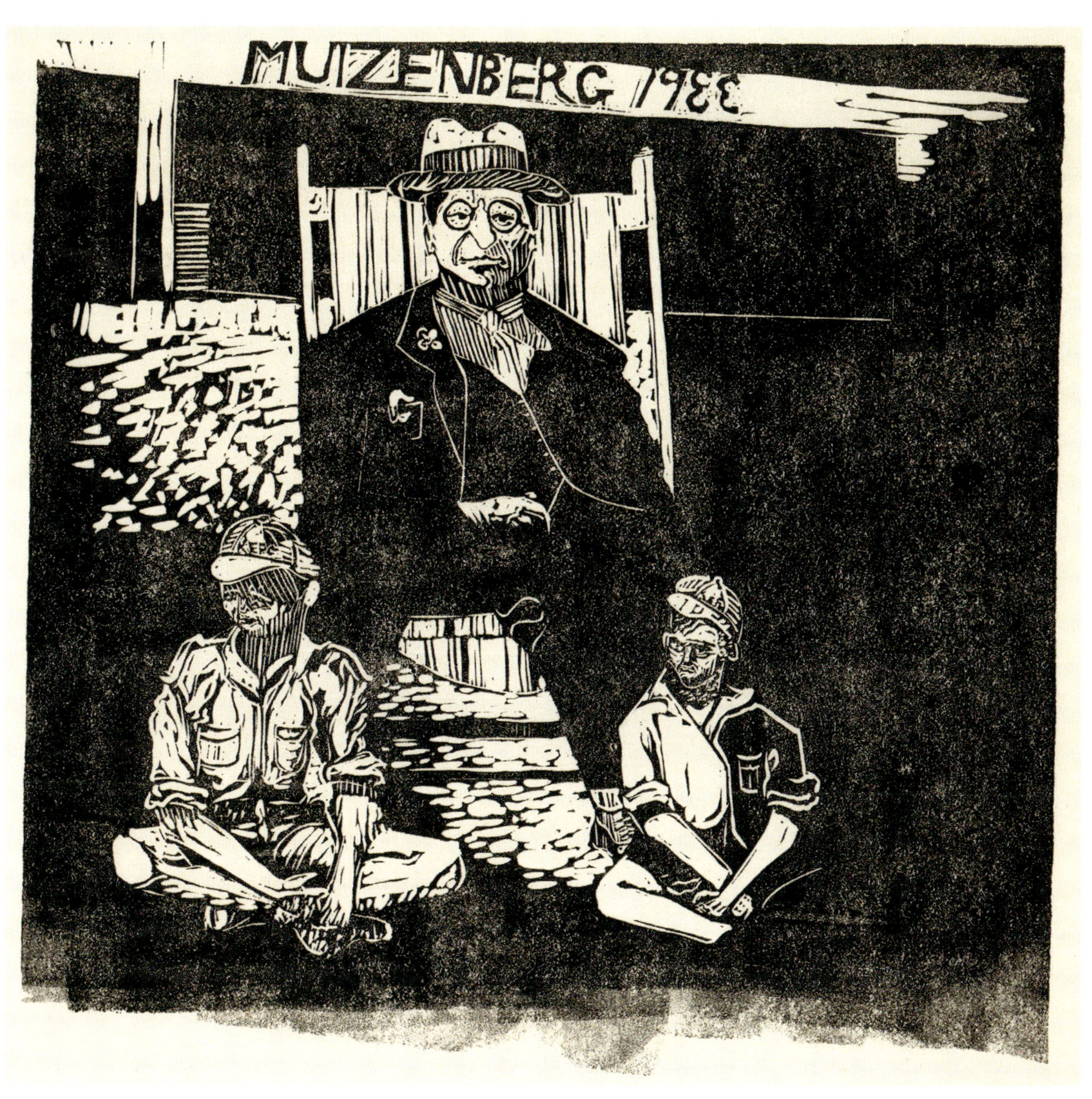

S.10.5 | linocut
image: 32 x 33 cm | sheet: 48 x 45 cm | paper: newsprint
edition: not editioned, although at least 4 impressions printed; 3 impressions identified at time of publishing
5th state: 1 figure missing

Muizenberg 1933

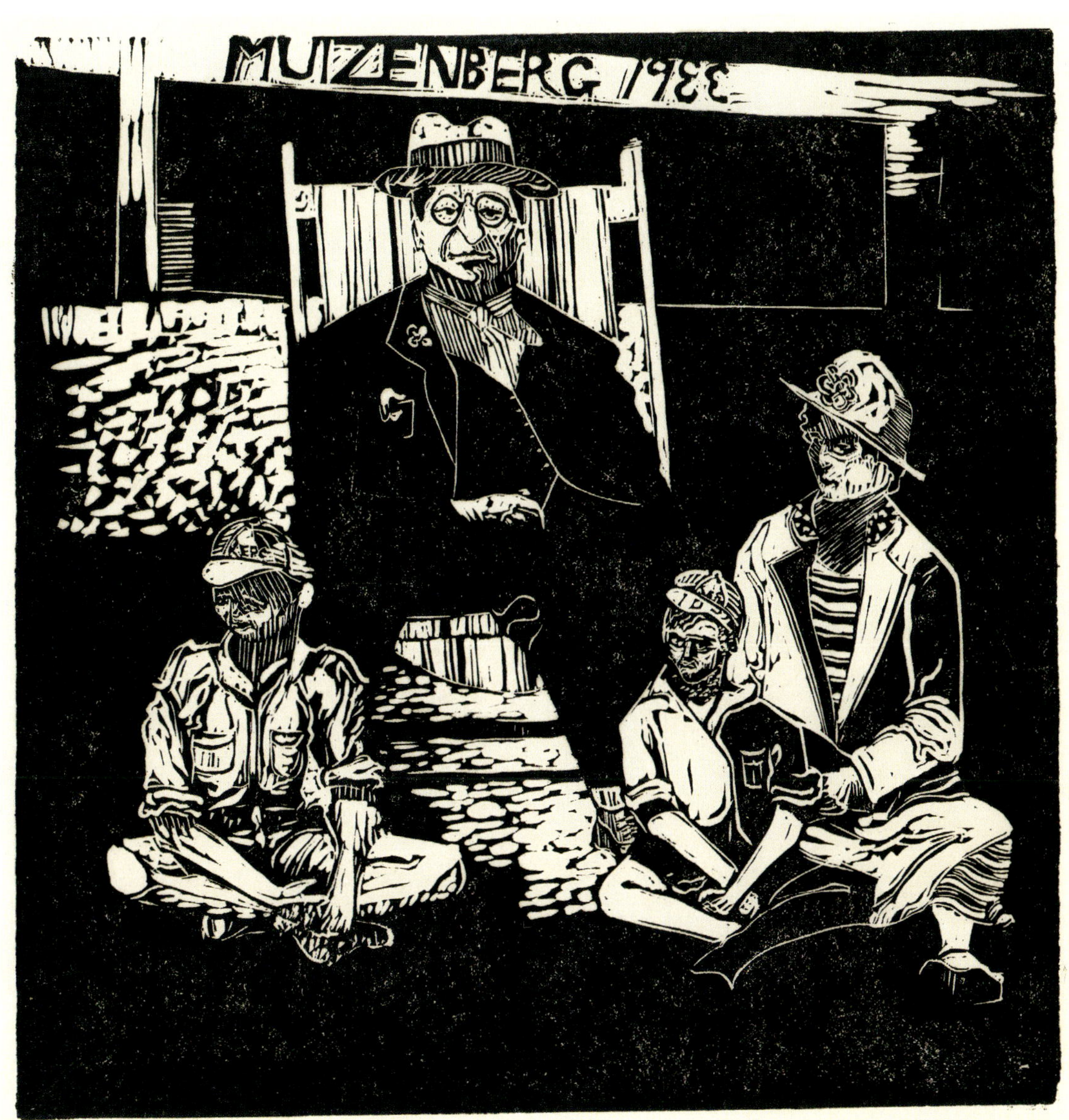

S.10.6 | linocut
image: 33 x 33 cm | sheet: 45.6 x 35.5 cm | paper: newsprint
edition: not editioned, although at least 10 impressions printed; 7 impressions identified at time of publishing
6th state: without bucket

WK : *In retrospect, this became an iconic image for me over many years and many projects, particularly the film* Tide Table *[2003] that shows the character Soho Eckstein in his pinstriped suit sitting in a deckchair on the beach, an image that comes very directly from this old family photograph of my grandfather, Morris Kentridge, in his Homburg and suit on the beach with my father, my uncle and a childminder seated on the sand next to them. Muizenberg was not my childhood holiday place but my father's site. I think there was something about the incongruity of the suit and the beach and the stripe of the deckchair, as well as the pinstripe of the suit; although in the print the stripes are only in the shirt and the deckchair. While making the print, I had no thought of animation, but after each few cuts I would do another test and pull another proof to see how the print was developing. In the end, there was a whole series of developing images, almost like a flip book that the image would form itself, much as the drawings did in the early animated films, such as* Johannesburg, 2nd Greatest City after Paris *[1989], that I made. So there is a retrospective look at the techniques and the nature of the prints, and there was a way I was being led by what they offered rather than me instructing the prints as to what they had to do, both in terms of technique and broader questions in terms of images. Images that I thought I chose almost at random, like this photograph, obviously had a much deeper connection to me inside, or else the deeper connection was forged through coming back to these images year after year. But it is one of the seminal images in the work of the past forty years.*

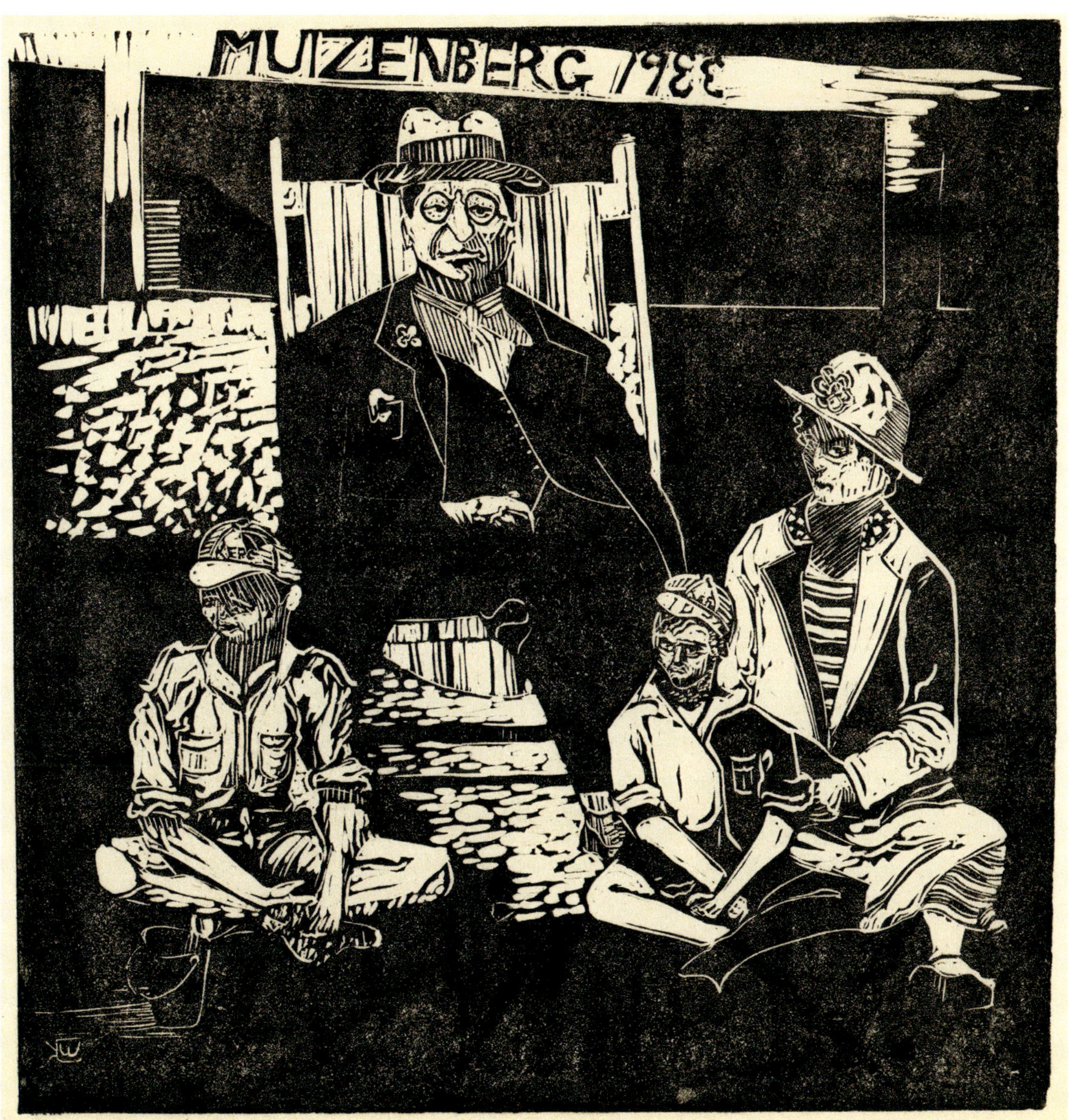

S.10.7 | reduction linocut
image: 33 x 32.6 cm | sheet: 35.5 x 45.5 cm | paper: newsprint and mulberry paper
edition: not editioned, although at least 10 impressions printed; 3 impressions identified at time of publishing
printer/publisher: William Kentridge, 72 Houghton Drive, Houghton, Johannesburg
signature style: signed 'WJK' in the plate; two impressions signed 'WJKentridge', c. 2019; some impressions unsigned
7th and final state: with bucket

Muizenberg 1933

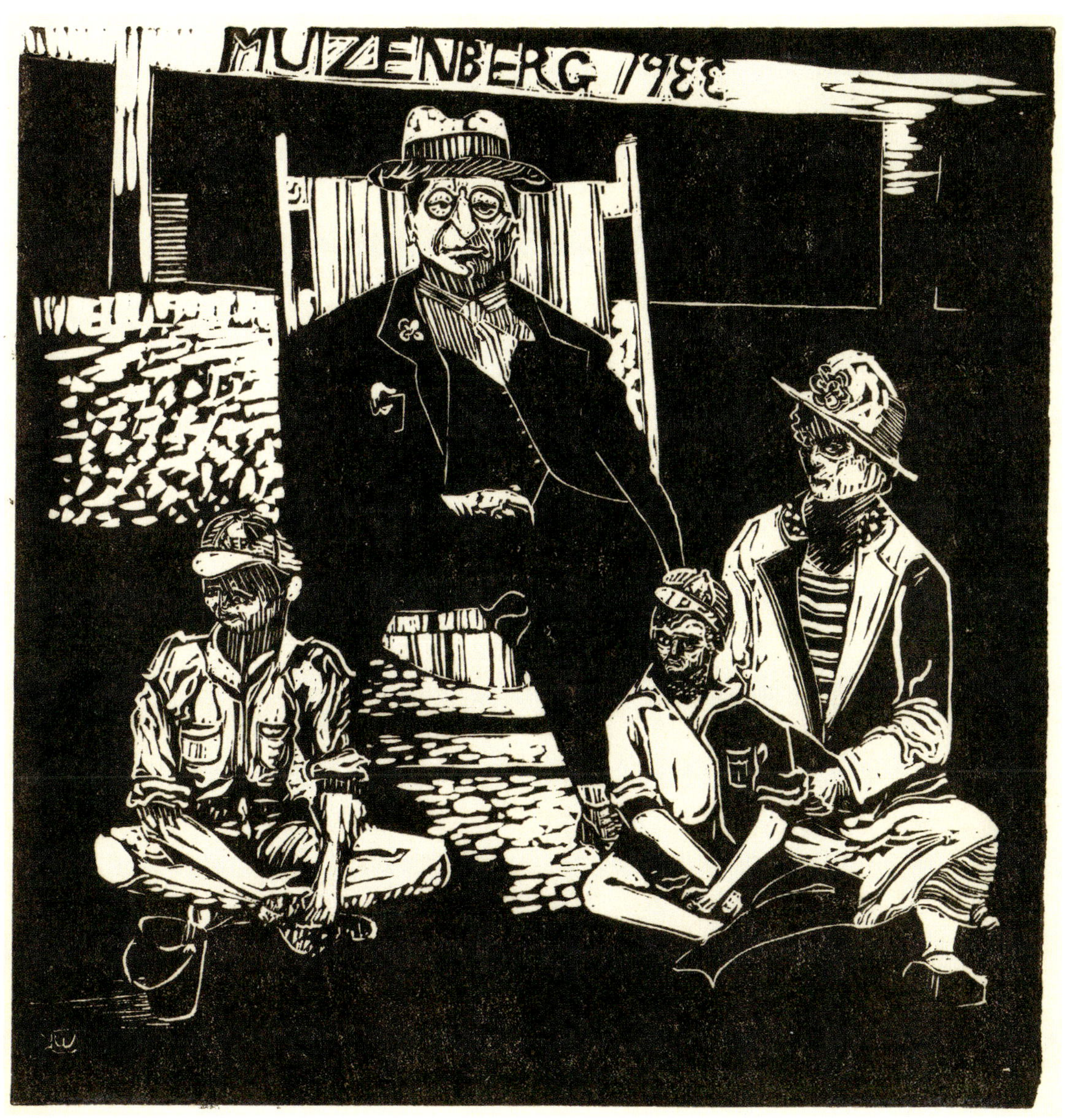

S.10.7i | colour reduction linocut
image: 33 x 32.6 cm | sheet: 46 x 35.5 cm | paper: newsprint
edition: unique impression
7th and final state, 1st variation: brown

Muizenberg 1933

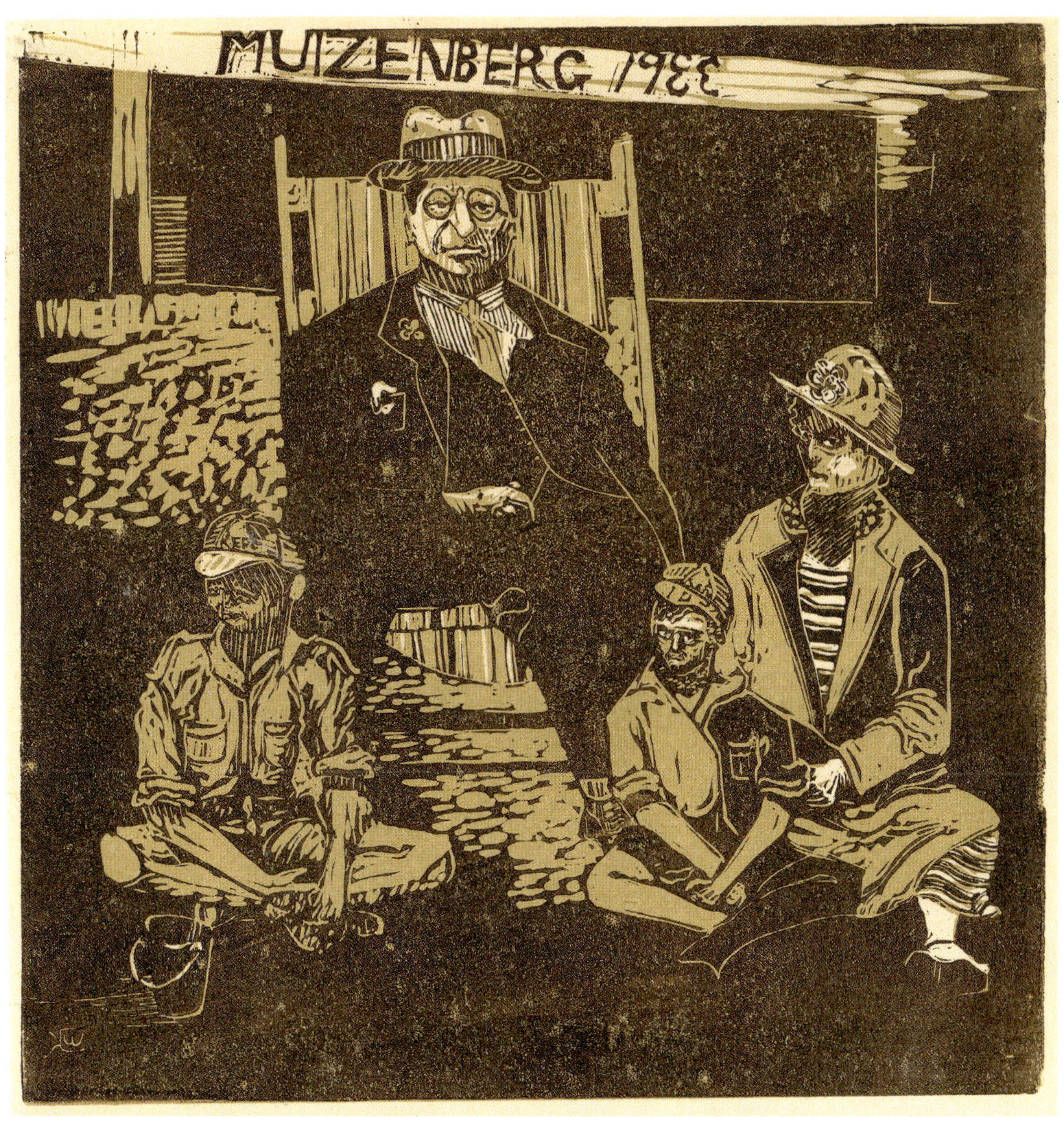

S.10.7ii | colour reduction linocut
image: 33 x 32.6 cm | sheet: 46 x 35.5 cm
paper: newsprint
edition: unique impression
7th and final state, 2nd variation: gold and brown

Already Dead Awaiting Stuffing

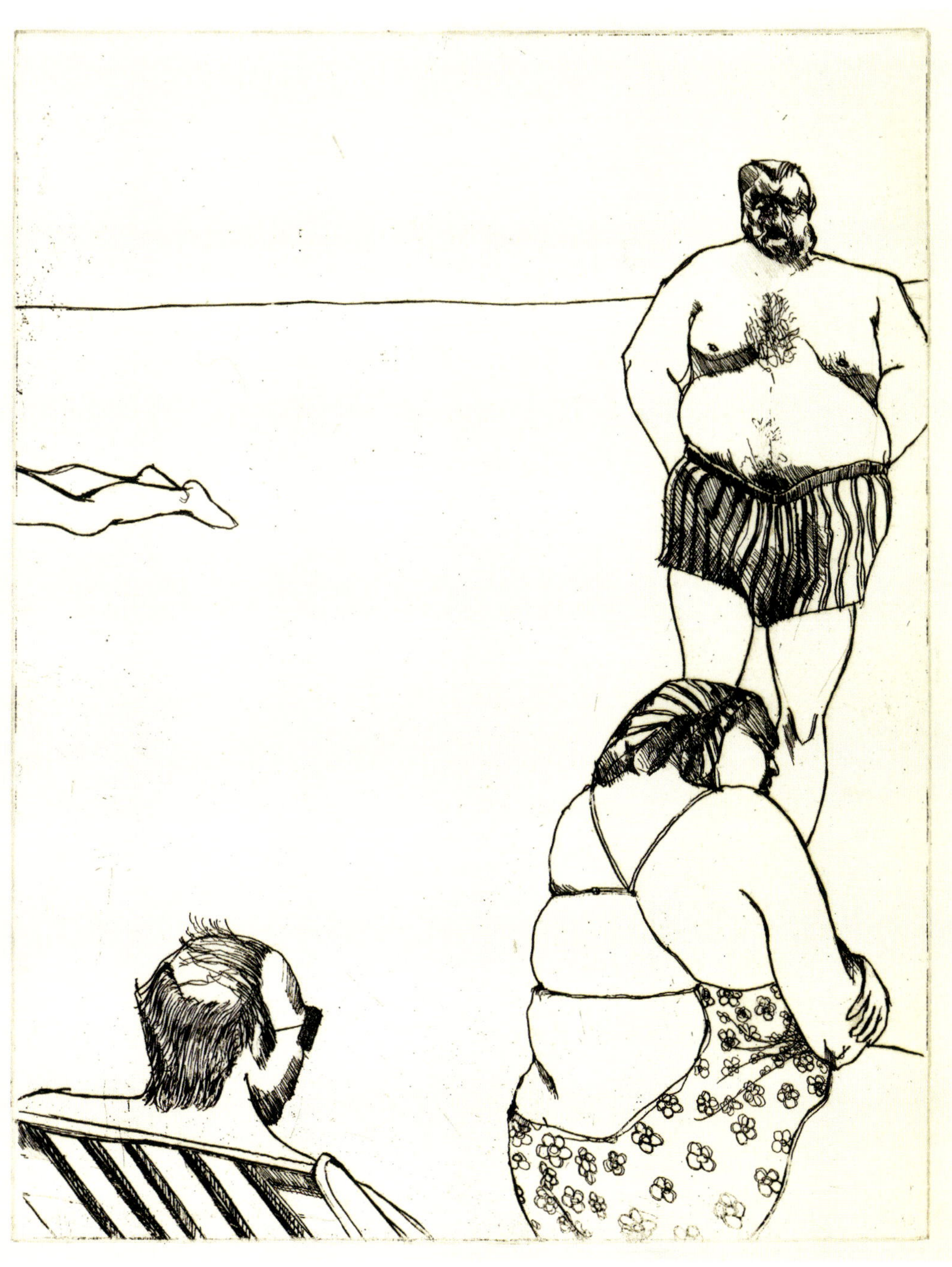

S.16.1 | etching
image: 25 x 19.8 cm | sheet: 33.5 x 33.5 cm | paper: Fabriano
edition: unique impression
1st state: without sky

Already Dead Awaiting Stuffing

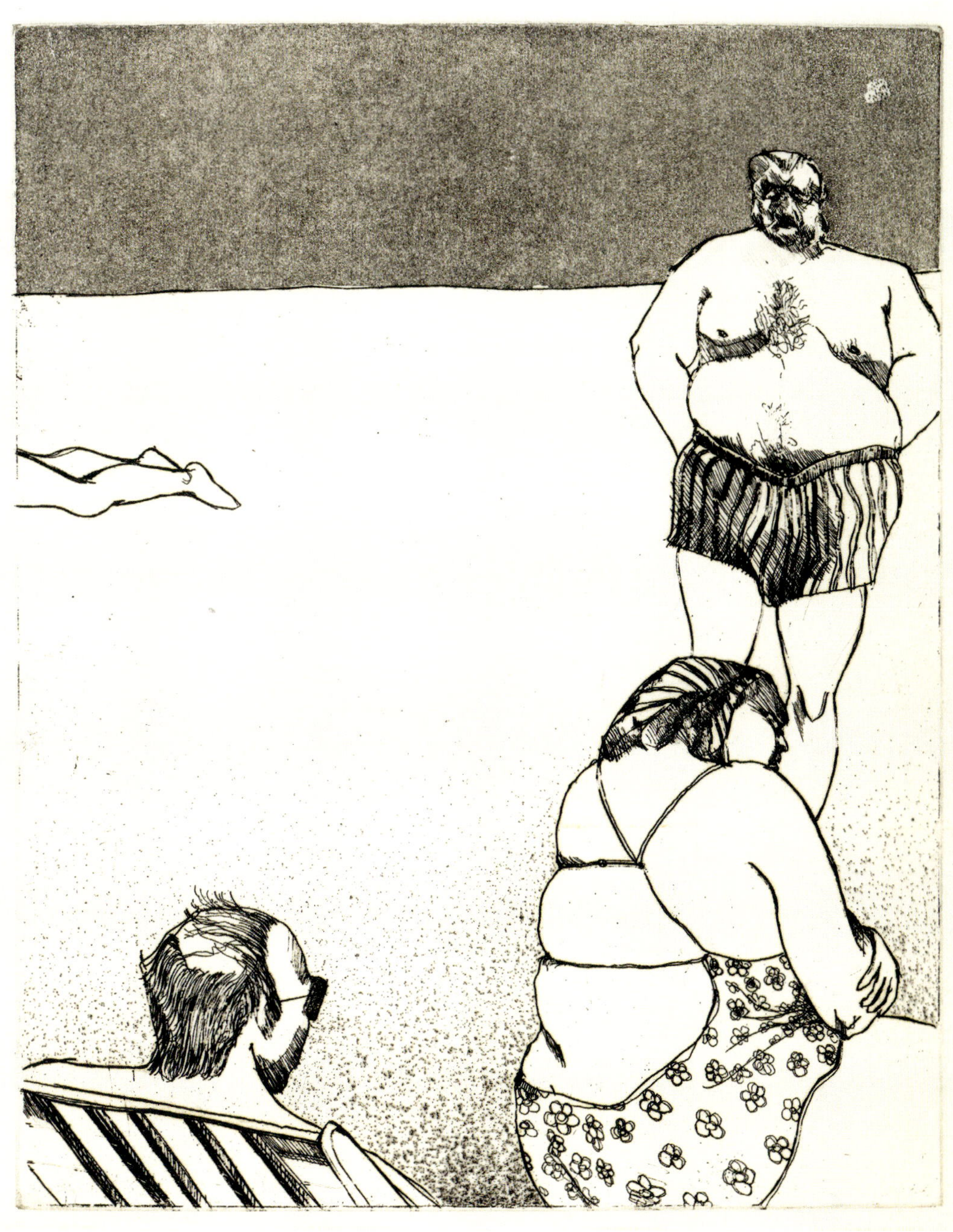

S.16.2 | etching
image: 25 x 19.8 cm | sheet: 35.8 x 34.5 cm | paper: Fabriano
edition: unique impression
2nd state: with sky

Already Dead Awaiting Stuffing

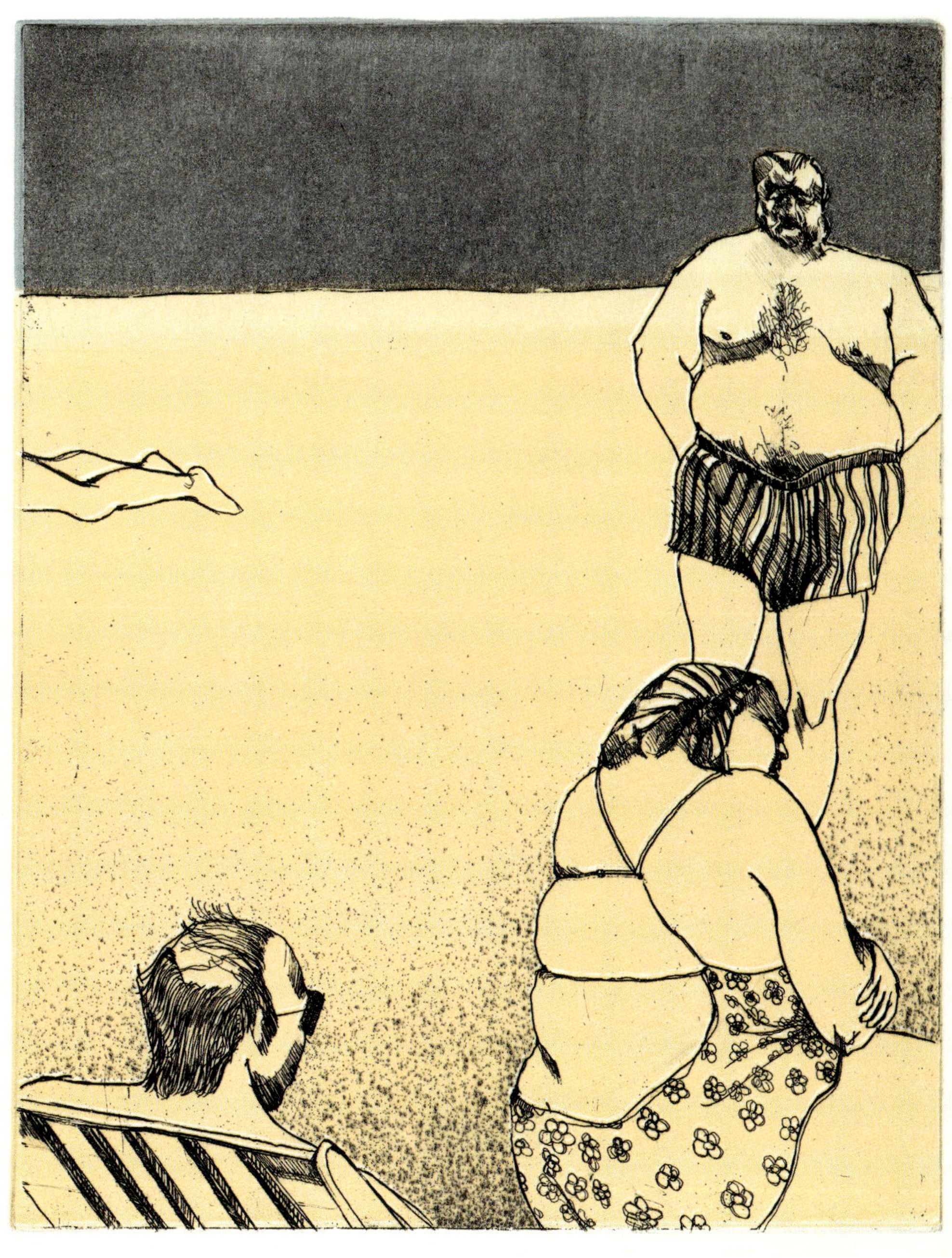

S.16.3 | etching
image: 25 x 19.8 cm | sheet: 35.5 x 34 cm | paper: Fabriano
edition: unique impression
3rd state: coloured beach and blue sky

WK : *This print was made at a one-week summer school that Pino Cattaneo ran at the University of the Witwatersrand [Wits]. The image was based on sketches of people on Muizenberg beach that I had done the year before, some of which also turned into a series of linocuts, in particular the man in the striped swimming costume [S. 20] and image with the striped deckchair [S. 17].*

The system that Pino used was both to do hard-ground etching but also to do a roll-up with colours with different degrees of grease in them to roll different colours on top of the plate with a tracing-paper stencil. So although it started as a hard ground, it had aquatint for the sky. I learned about that technique from him. The heart of what he was interested in at that stage was also the coloured stencils of the print—the pink of the swimming costume, the variegated colour of the sky that was rolled up, the colour of the beach. In fact, of the four days of the summer-school workshop, two days were spent on the burnishing and grinding and filing of the edges of the plate, something which never took as long ever again, but which was a good discipline for those days. On the strength of this one week of summer school of making one etching plate, which included hard ground and aquatint and roll-up colours, I started the etching department at Ainslie's Studios and was rescued in my teaching by the assistance of Rosanna Mahony, an artist from England who had done four years of printmaking, and she taught me a great deal, particularly techniques of colour printing and soft-ground etching.

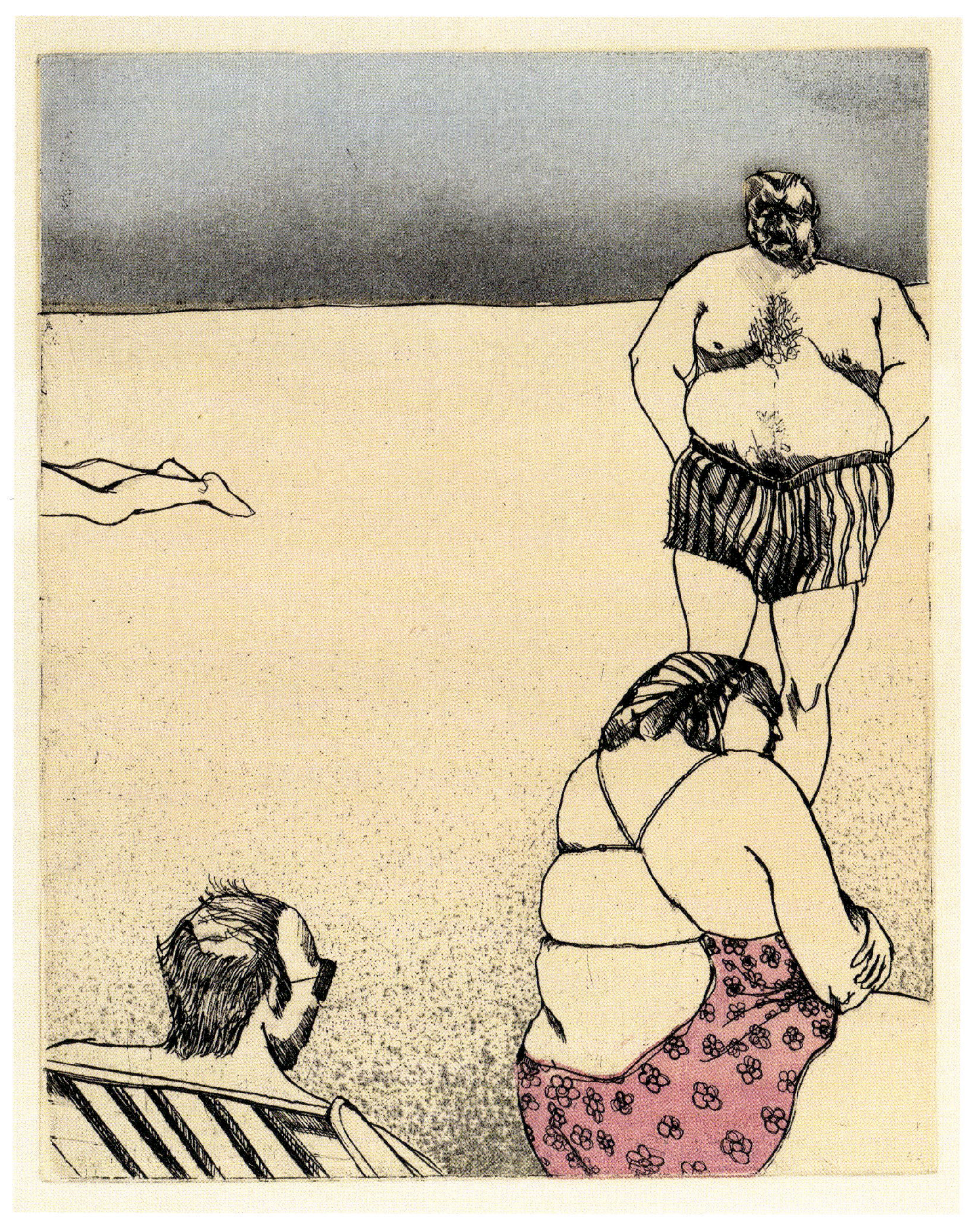

S.16.4 | etching and aquatint
image: 24.5 x 19.8 cm | sheet: 36 x 31.3 cm | paper: Fabriano
edition: not editioned, although at least 6 impressions printed; 4 impressions identified at time of publishing
printer/publisher: William Kentridge, University of the Witwatersrand, Johannesburg
signature style: WJK '77; some impressions unsigned
4th and final state: pink swimming costume

Muizenberg Beach–Old Man Seated in Deckchair*

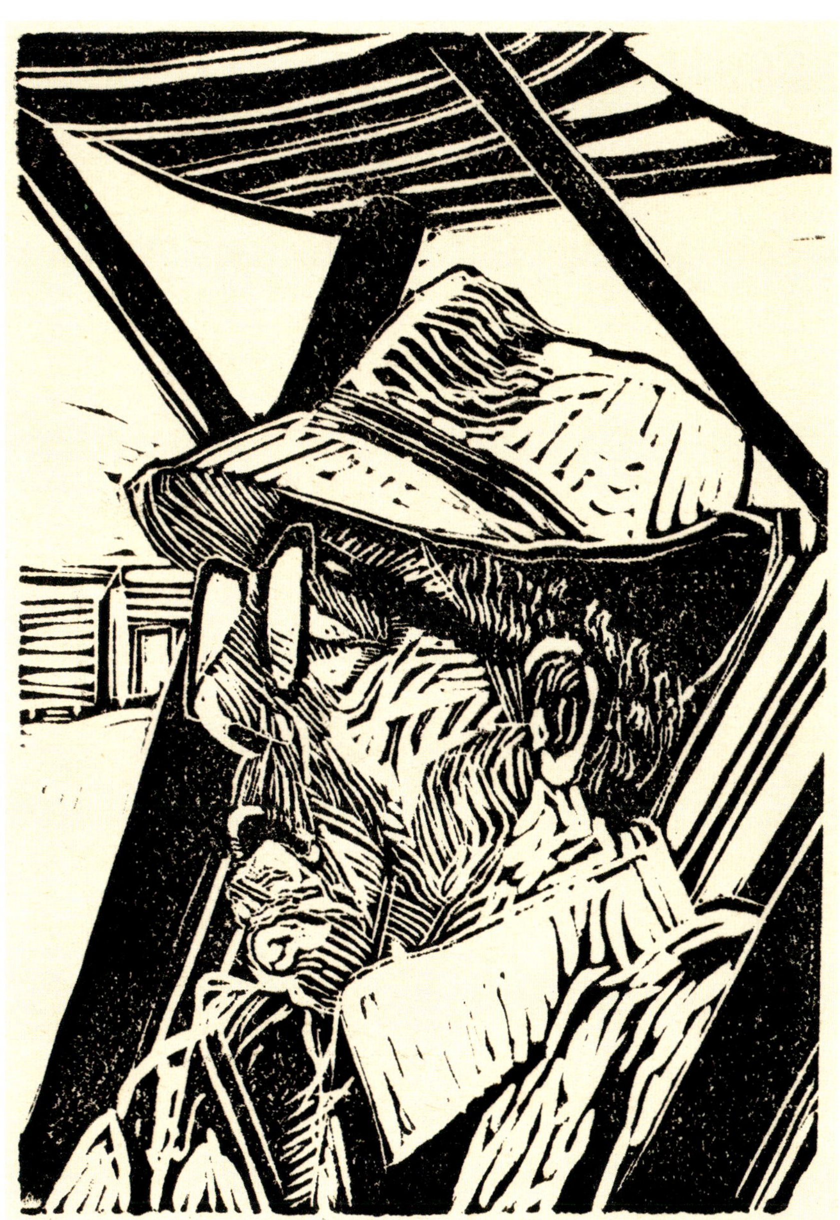

S.17.1 | linocut
image: 18 x 12.6 cm | sheet: 27.5 x 18.5 cm | paper: newsprint
edition: unique impression
1st state: shade cloth extends to top-left corner with no sky visible

Muizenberg Beach–Old Man Seated in Deckchair*

WK : *One can see the same man in the deckchair from the Muizenberg etching referenced again in this linocut. These were reductive linocuts where different areas are successively cut away, so the entire edition would be printed in one session. I think the colour must have been a separate block. They were very small editions, maybe as little as five, but it was never formally an edition. These were based on sketches I had made in situ in Muizenberg in December 1975 or January 1976.*

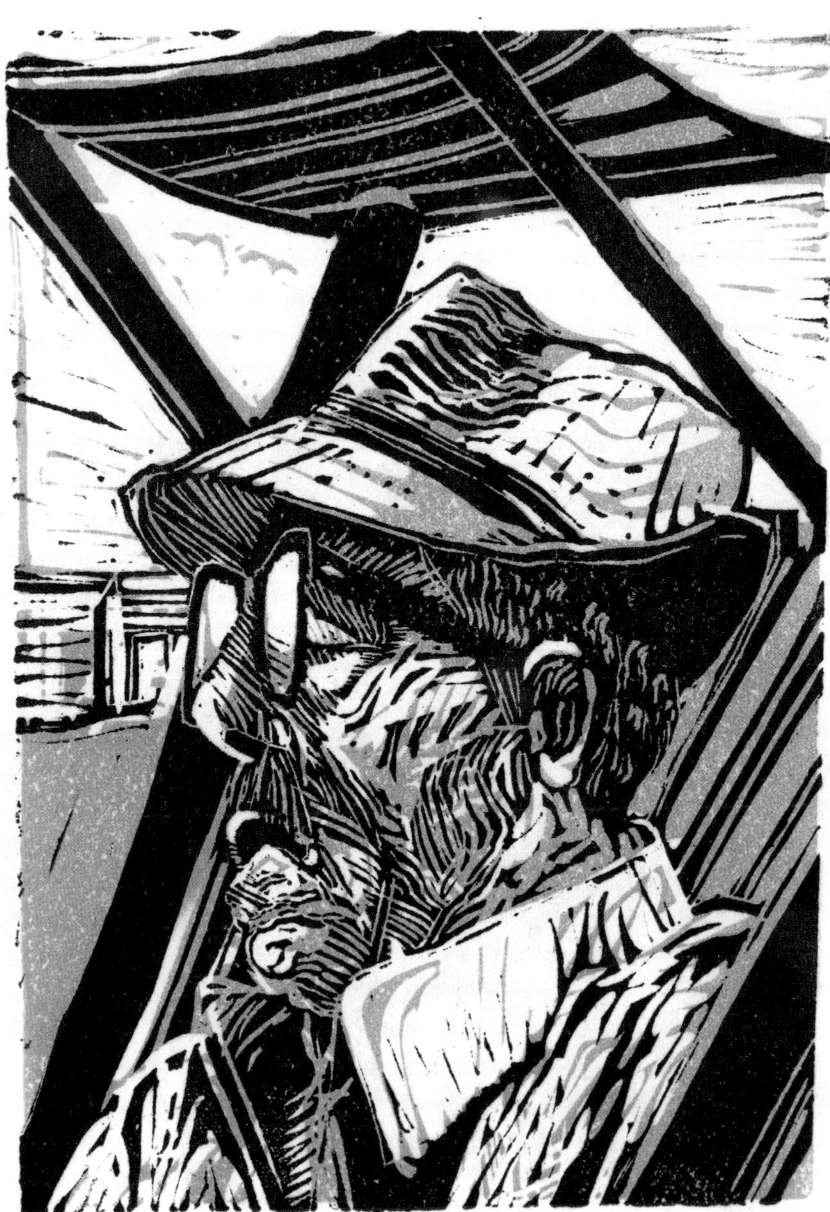

S.17.2 | colour reduction linocut
image: 18 x 12.6 cm | sheet varies: 27.5 x 18.5 cm to 46.5 x 31 cm | paper: mulberry paper
edition: not editioned, although at least 5 impressions printed; 3 impressions identified at time of publishing
printer/publisher: William Kentridge, Ainslie's Studios, Saxonwold, Johannesburg
signature style: WJK '77; some impressions unsigned
2nd and final state: with addition of colour and sky detail in top-left corner

Muizenberg Beach–Man Wearing Sunglasses and Beach Hat*

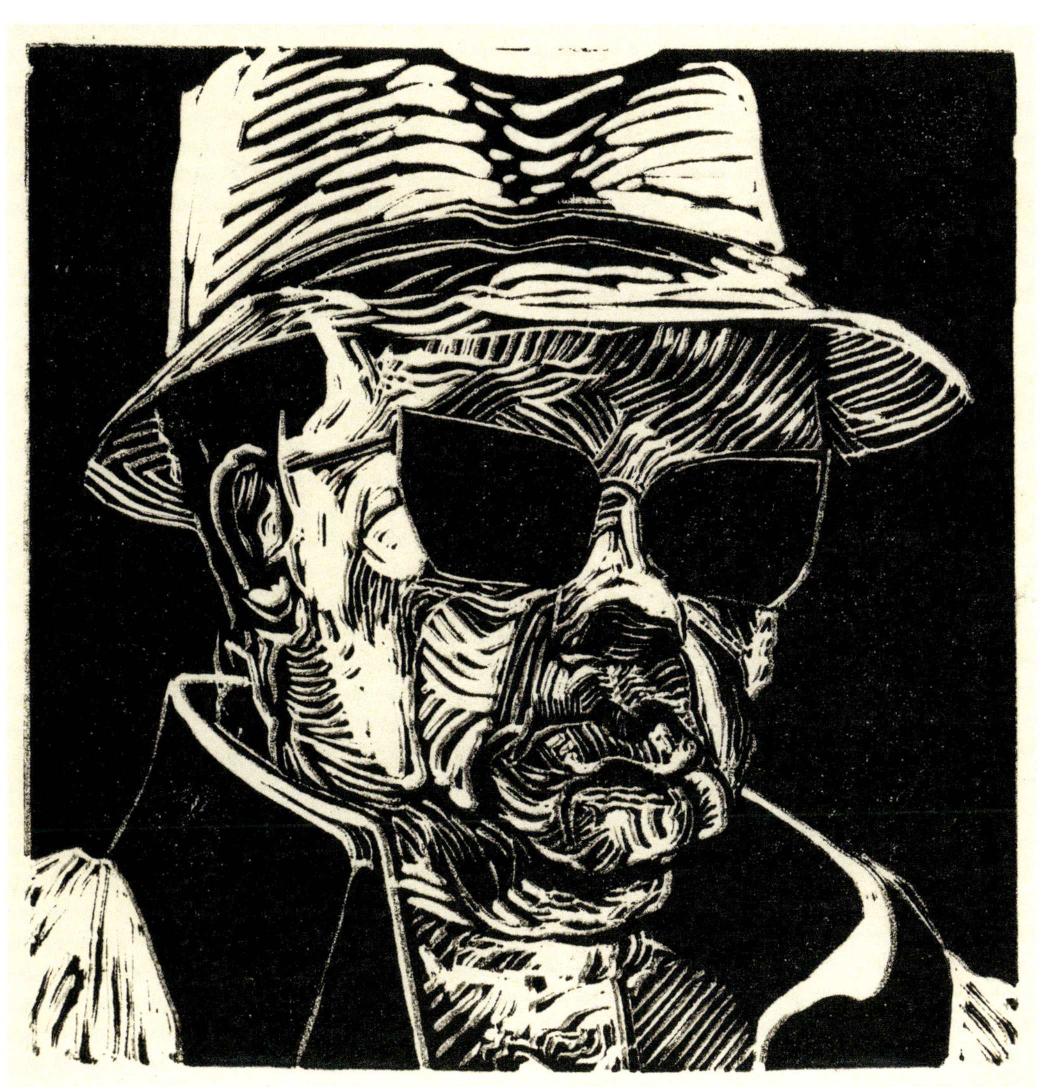

S.18.1 | linocut
image: 15.3 x 15.3 cm | sheet: 35.5 x 23 cm | paper: newsprint
edition: not editioned, although at least 3 impressions printed; 2 impressions identified at time of publishing
1st state: solid background without colour

Muizenberg Beach–Man Wearing Sunglasses and Beach Hat*

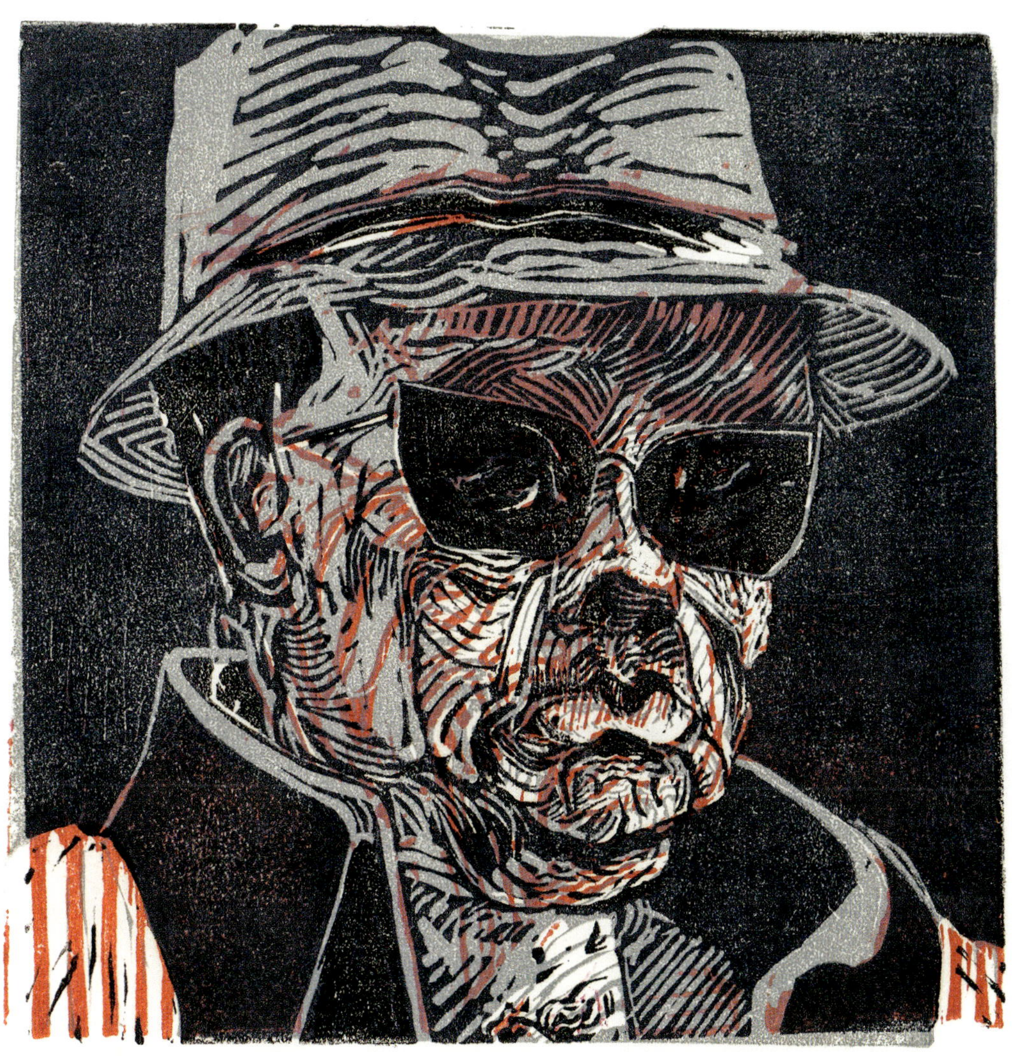

S.18.2 | colour reduction linocut
image: 15.3 x 15.3 cm | sheet: 31.8 x 23.5 cm | paper: mulberry paper
edition: not editioned, although at least 5 impressions printed; 4 impressions identified at time of publishing
2nd state: solid background with colour

Muizenberg Beach—Man Wearing Sunglasses and Beach Hat*

WK : *Here I was still trying to work out how a face should be cut: how much detail,
how little detail, how naturalistic. So something like the black of the dark sunglasses
was a relief in that it answered that question itself. I think the colours must have been
a separate block, probably the grey and the red from one block of linoleum. You can see
that the registration along the bottom right-hand corner between the different plates
is not perfect by any means. At this stage I was still trying to see how one could use
colour in printmaking. The third state, where the sky has been cut away and the hat
simplified, shows a process gradually finding a form within the image.*

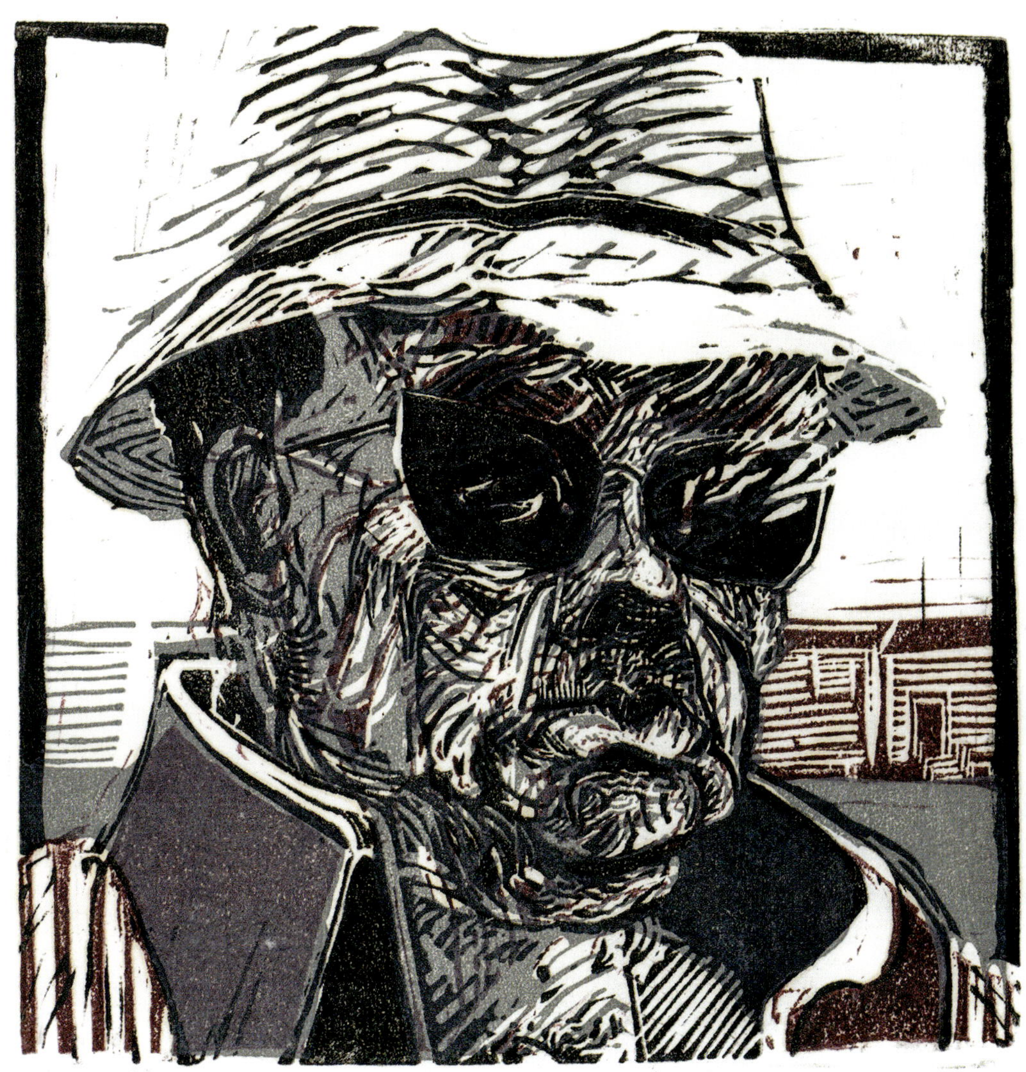

S18.3 | colour reduction linocut
image: 15.3 x 15.3 cm | sheet: 31.8 x 23.5 cm | paper: mulberry paper
edition: not editioned, although at least 5 impressions printed; 3 impressions identified at time of publishing
printer/publisher: William Kentridge, Ainslie's Studios, Saxonwold, Johannesburg
signature style: WJK '77; some impressions unsigned
3rd and final state: with houses

Muizenberg Beach–Man with Sunglasses*

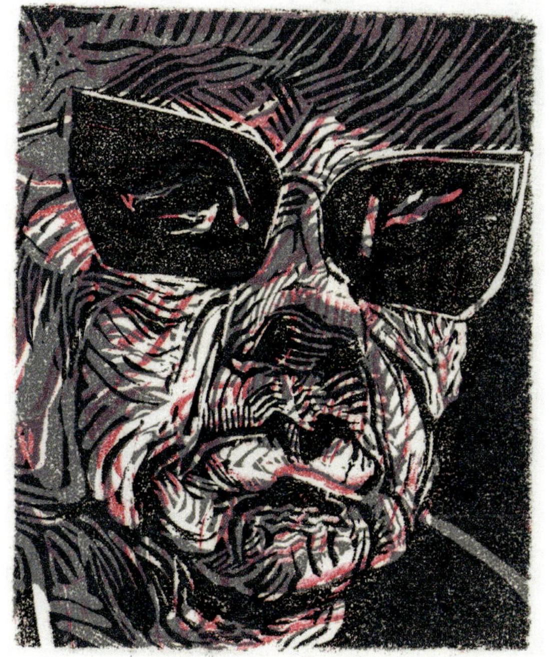

S.19 | colour linocut
image: 8.8 x 7.3 cm | sheet: 23.5 x 16 cm | paper: mulberry paper
edition: 4 impressions, 2 APs; 4 impressions identified at time of publishing
printer/publisher: William Kentridge, Ainslie's Studios, Saxonwold, Johannesburg
signature style: WJK '77, WJK 2/77; some impressions unsigned

Muizenberg Beach–Man with Arms Behind his Back*

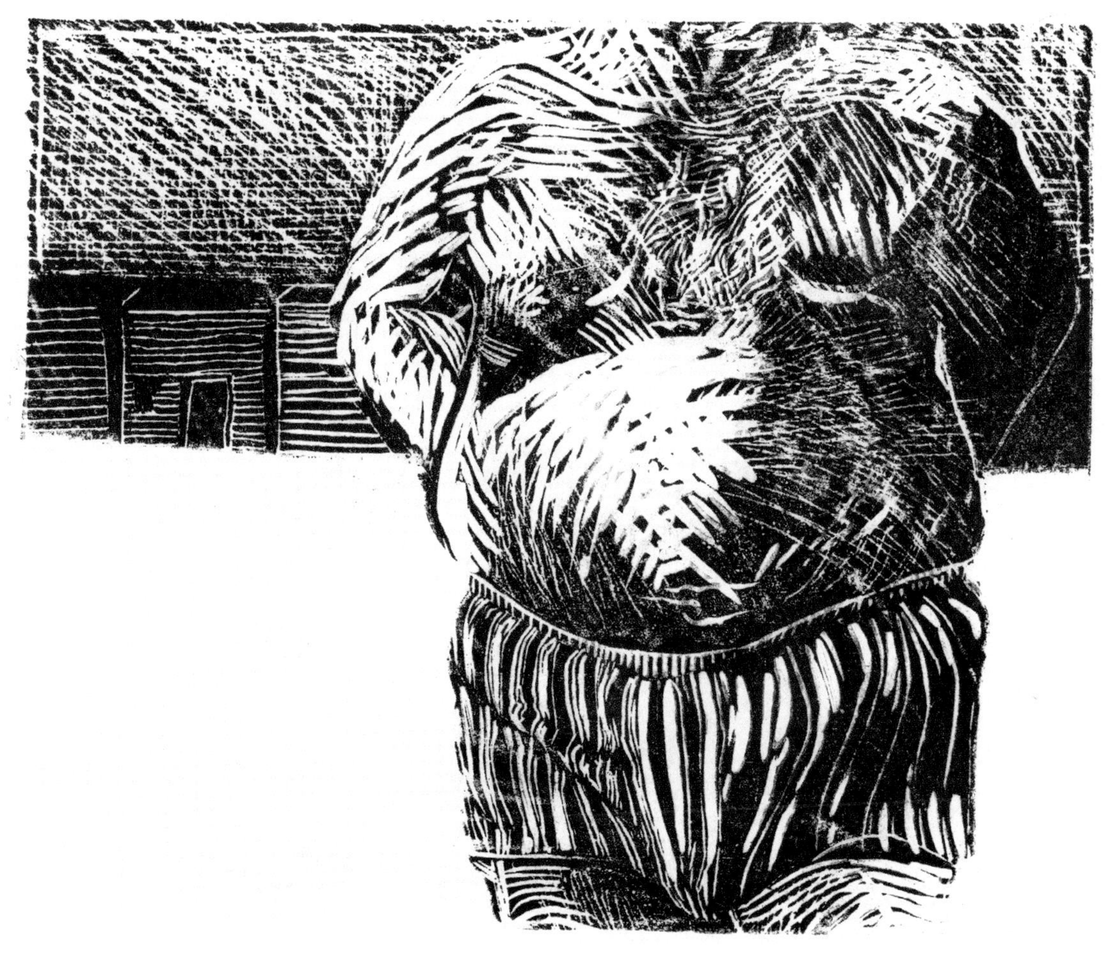

S.20.1 | linocut
image: 17 x 20.5 cm | sheet: 28.7 x 28 cm | paper: mulberry paper
edition: unique impression
1st state: blank beach

Muizenberg Beach–Man with Arms Behind his Back*

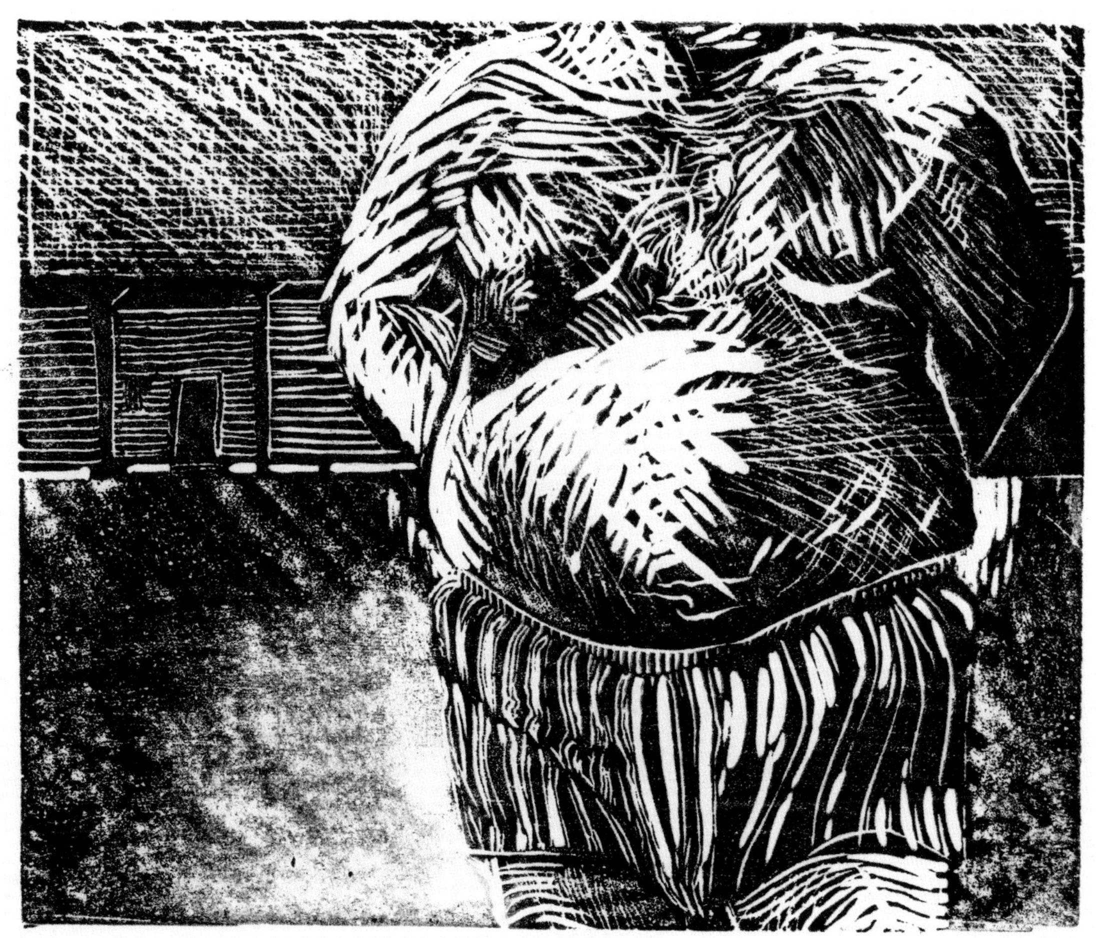

S.20.2 | linocut and caustic soda
image: 17 x 20.5 cm | sheet: 31.5 x 32 cm | paper: mulberry paper
edition: not editioned, although at least 5 impressions printed; 4 impressions identified at time of publishing
2nd state: definition added to beach

Muizenberg Beach–Man with Arms Behind his Back*

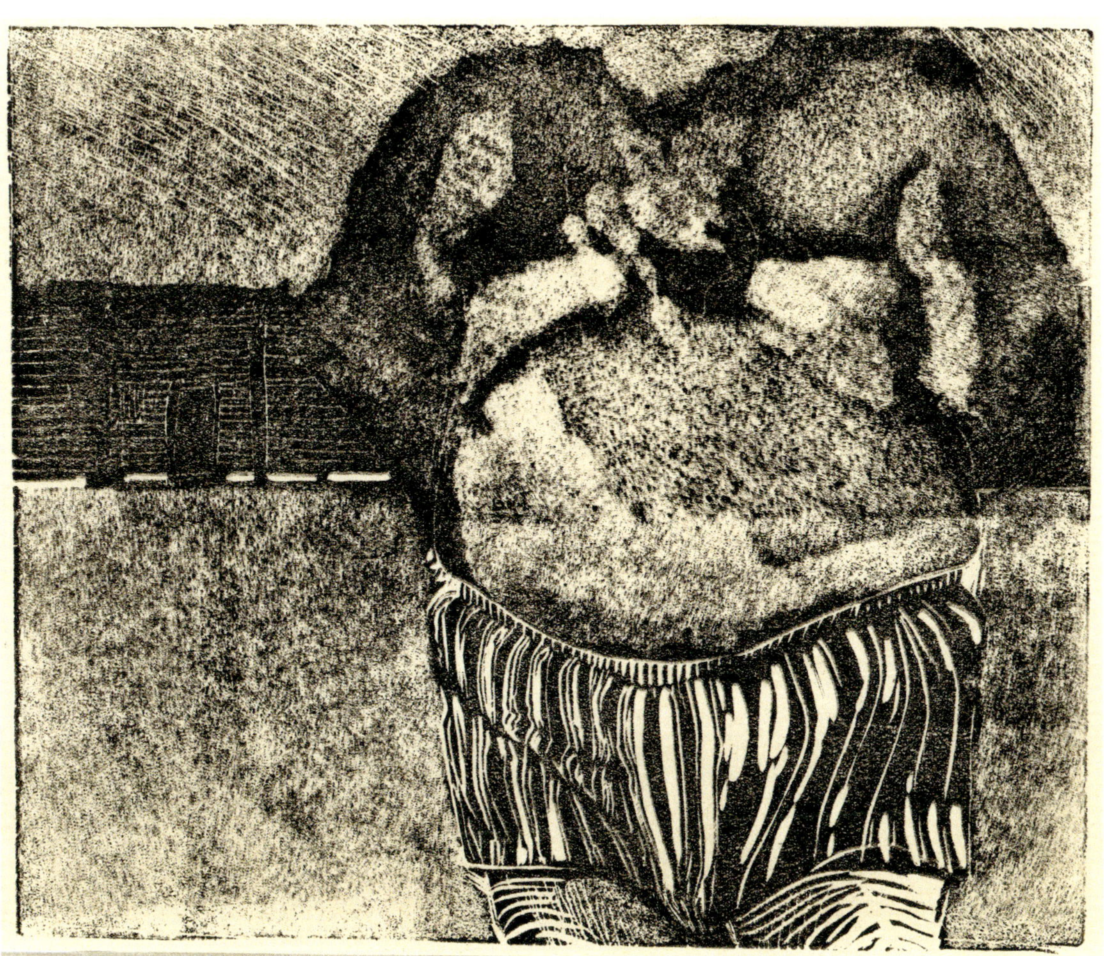

S.20.3 | linocut and caustic soda
image: 17 x 20.5 cm | sheet: 17.8 x 22.8 cm | paper: newsprint
edition: unique impression
3rd state: loss of background definition

Muizenberg Beach–Man with Arms Behind his Back*

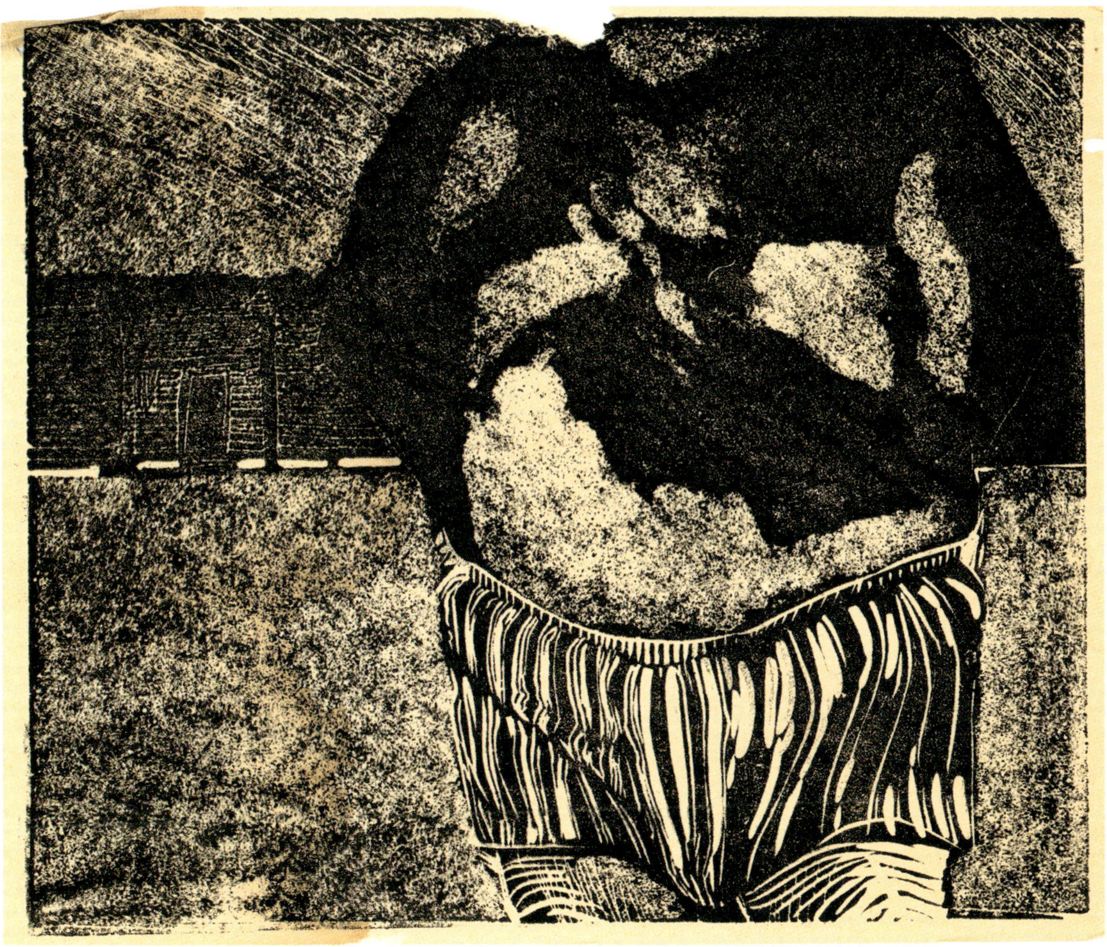

S.20.4 | linocut and caustic soda
image: 17 x 20.5 cm | sheet: 17.7 x 22.9 cm | paper: newsprint
edition: unique impression
4th state: darkening of upper body

Muizenberg Beach–Man with Arms Behind his Back*

WK : *This is also part of the Muizenberg series. Someone at Ainslie's Studios had told me about a way of doing a kind of aquatint on a linoleum block using caustic soda, as the acid eats away unevenly at the surface. Depending on how long you left the caustic soda on the linoleum surface, more or less would be eaten away, giving you a bright white [as on the belly of the man in the image], or less bright [as in the beach and the sky behind him]. What I hadn't realised is that it was hard to stop the action of the caustic soda, and the block itself became very unstable. If there was a way of stabilising it, I never learnt it. So there would always be a couple of good prints, and then the blacks would get too black and the mid-tones would disappear. You can see in the third state that I used two separate blocks. I used the trousers of the one, probably stopped out with tracing paper, to block out the rest of the image when inking up the plate, so that only the bathing costume and legs were printed [leaving the beach blank]. The second state is a combination of two blocks, and the third state is fuzzier, having been eaten by the caustic soda. It would not have been possible to achieve the visual clarity of states one and two once the linoleum block had been exposed to the caustic soda. It was probably a tracing of the same image on two blocks, which is why they seem so similar.*

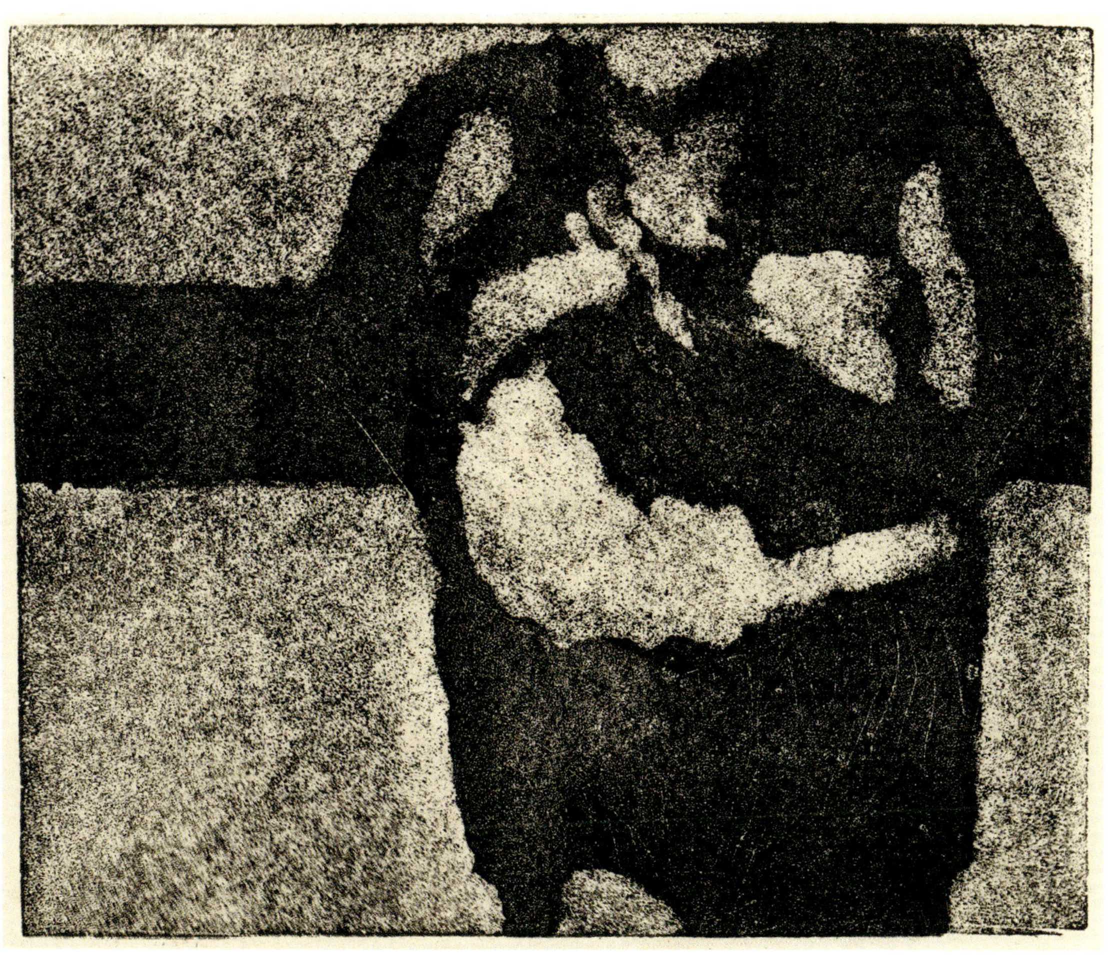

S.20.5 | linocut and caustic soda
image: 17 x 20.5 cm | sheet: 17.8 x 23 cm | paper: newsprint
edition: not editioned, although at least 3 impressions printed; 2 impressions identified at time of publishing
printer/publisher: William Kentridge, Ainslie's Studios, Saxonwold, Johannesburg
signature style: WJK '77, WJKentridge, c. 2018; some impressions unsigned
5th and final state: near-solid beach huts and bathing costume

Muizenberg Beach—Woman on Towel with Sunglasses*

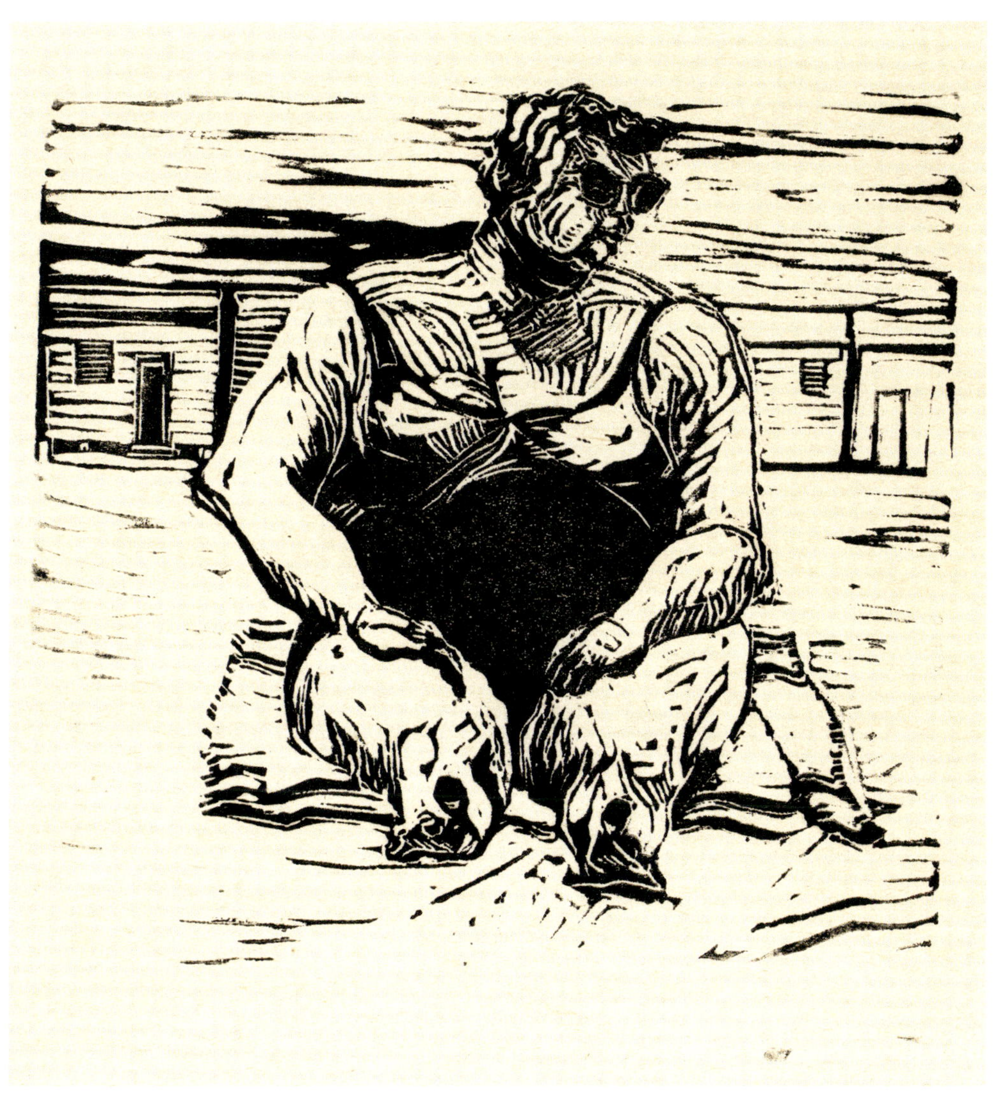

S.21.1 | linocut
image: 14 x 14.8 cm | sheet: 35.5 x 22.8 cm | paper: newsprint
edition: unique impression
1st state: printed in black only

Muizenberg Beach–Woman on Towel with Sunglasses*

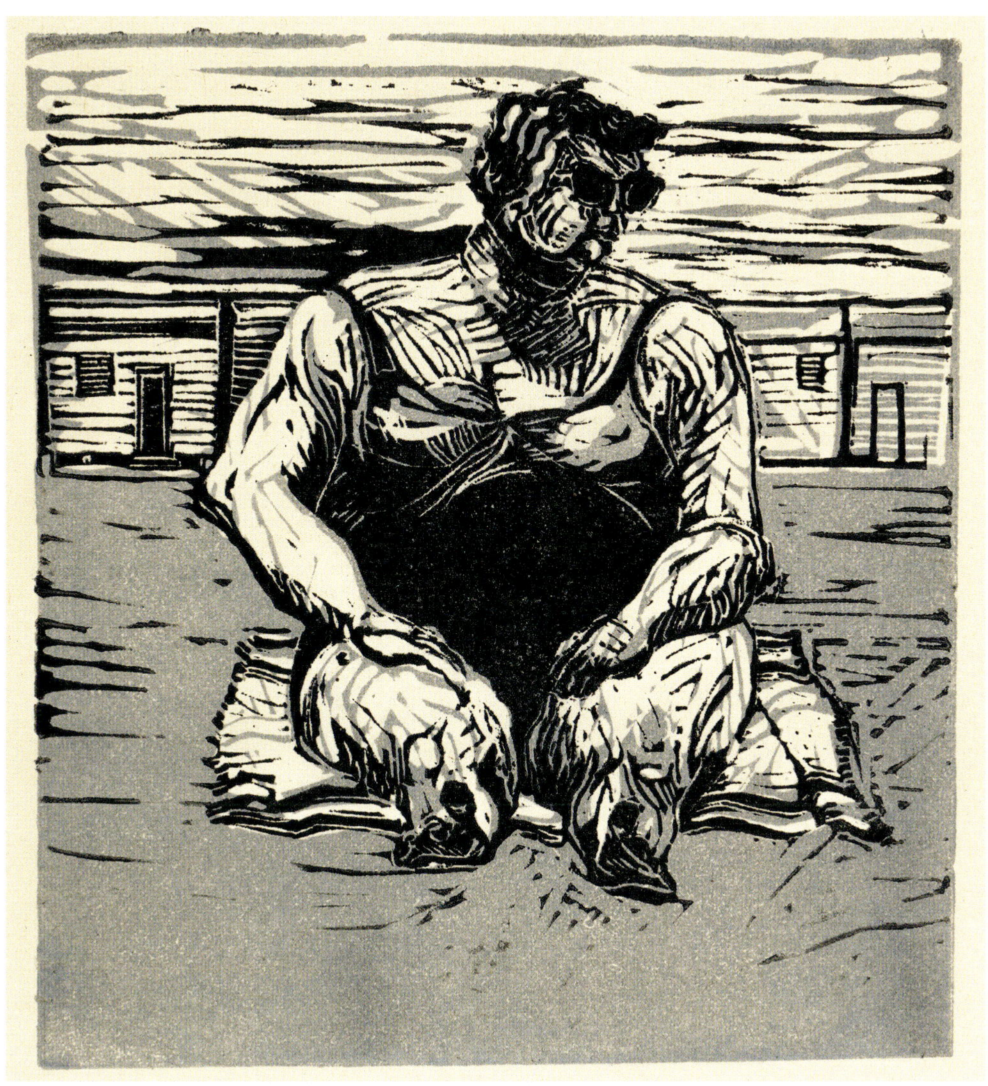

S.21.2i | colour reduction linocut
image: 16.3 x 15 cm | sheet: 27.5 x 23.5 cm | paper: newsprint
edition: unique impression
2nd state: colour variation printed in black and blue

Muizenberg Beach–Woman on Towel with Sunglasses*

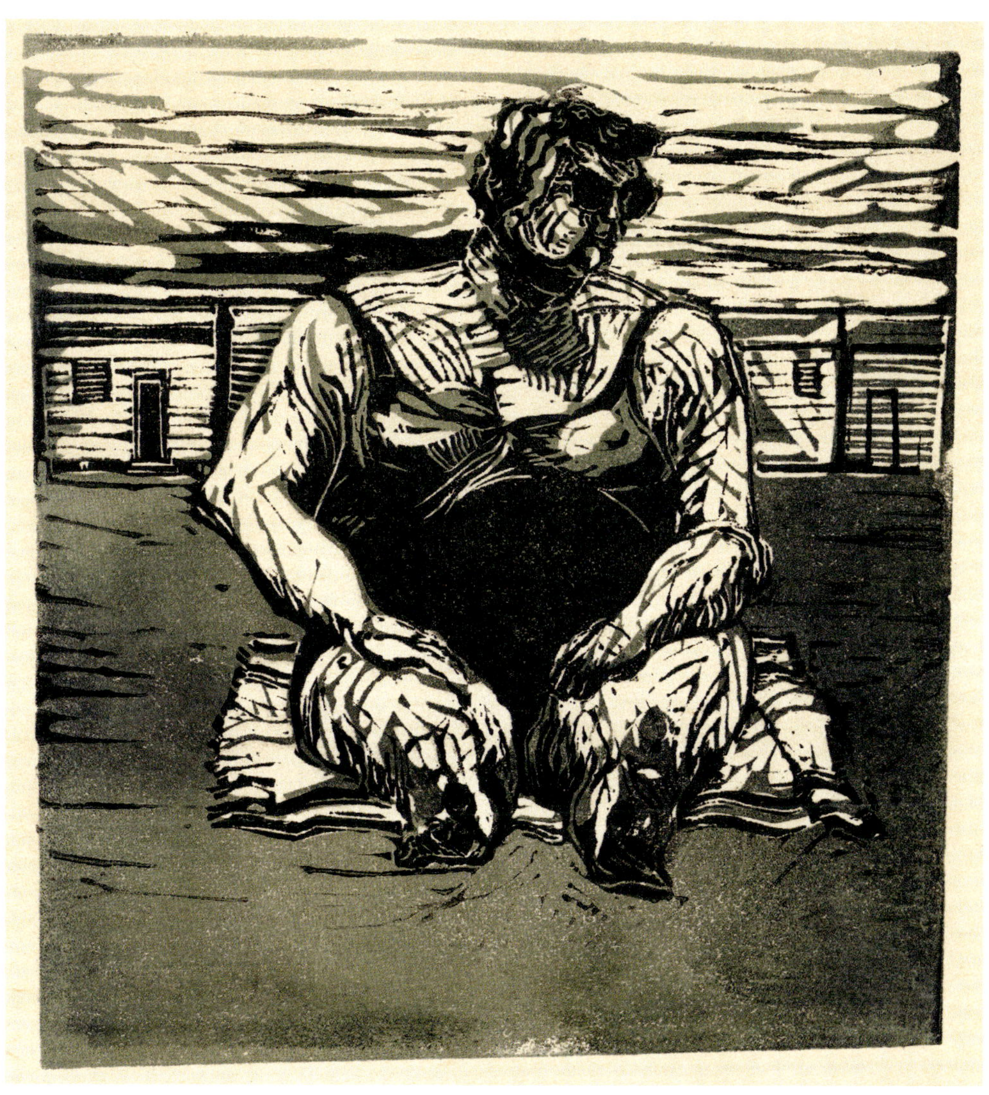

S.21.2ii | colour reduction linocut
image: 16.3 x 15 cm | sheet: 35.5 x 23 cm | paper: newsprint
edition: unique impression
2nd state, 1st variation: colour variation printed in black and green

Muizenberg Beach–Woman on Towel with Sunglasses*

WK : *The woman on the beach also has the black sunglasses and the black costume to give her that clarity of image. It would have been made using two different blocks— one with the black, the second one with the light grey, printed on top of each other. You can see that the registration of the black and grey are not perfect, as it was printed using these two blocks. At that point, if I thought I could get registration to about three or four millimetres, it was certainly accurate enough. All the prints were made with that in mind.*

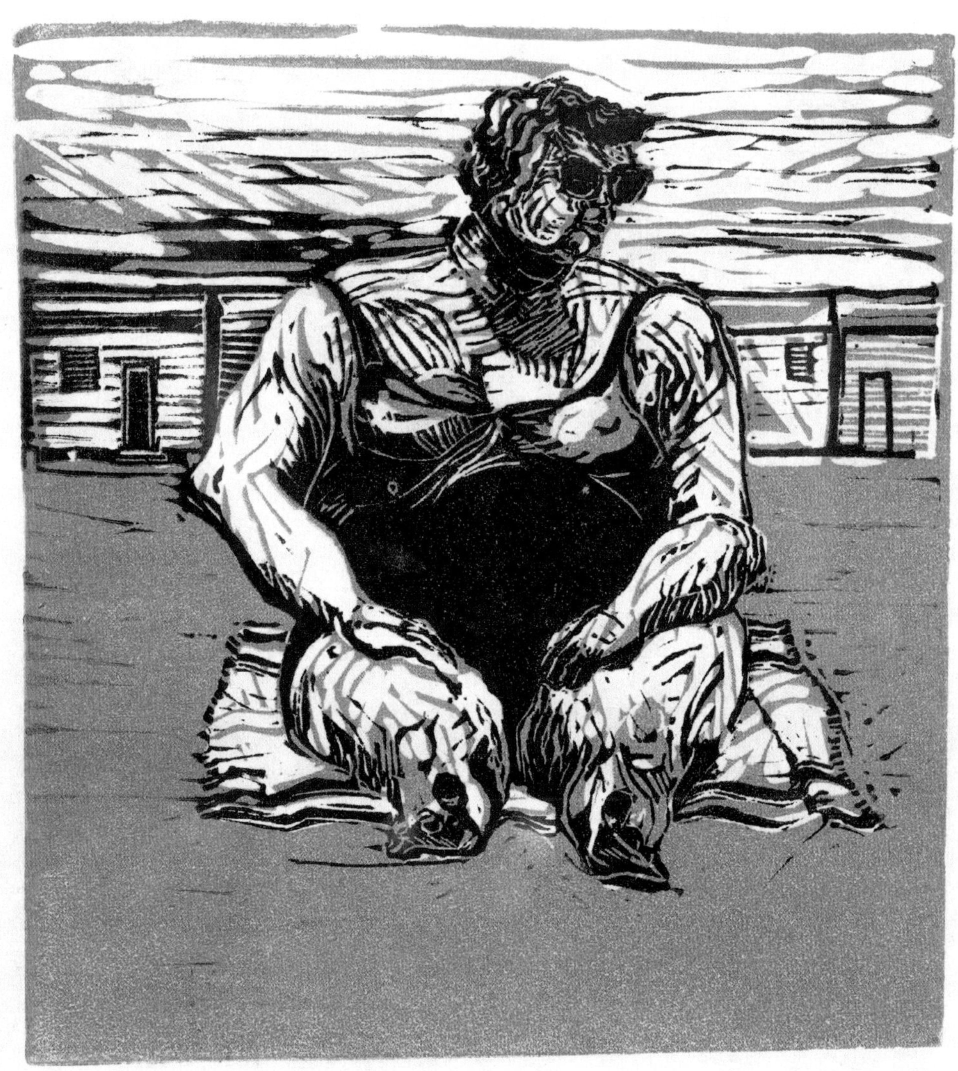

S.21.3 | colour reduction linocut
image: 16.3 x 15 cm | sheet: 26.2 x 26.6 cm | paper: mulberry paper
edition: not editioned, although at least 5 impressions printed; 1 impression identified at time of publishing
printer/publisher: William Kentridge, Ainslie's Studios, Saxonwold, Johannesburg
signature style: WJK '77; some impressions unsigned
3rd and final state: reduced beach detail

Muizenberg Beach–Bathing Hut*

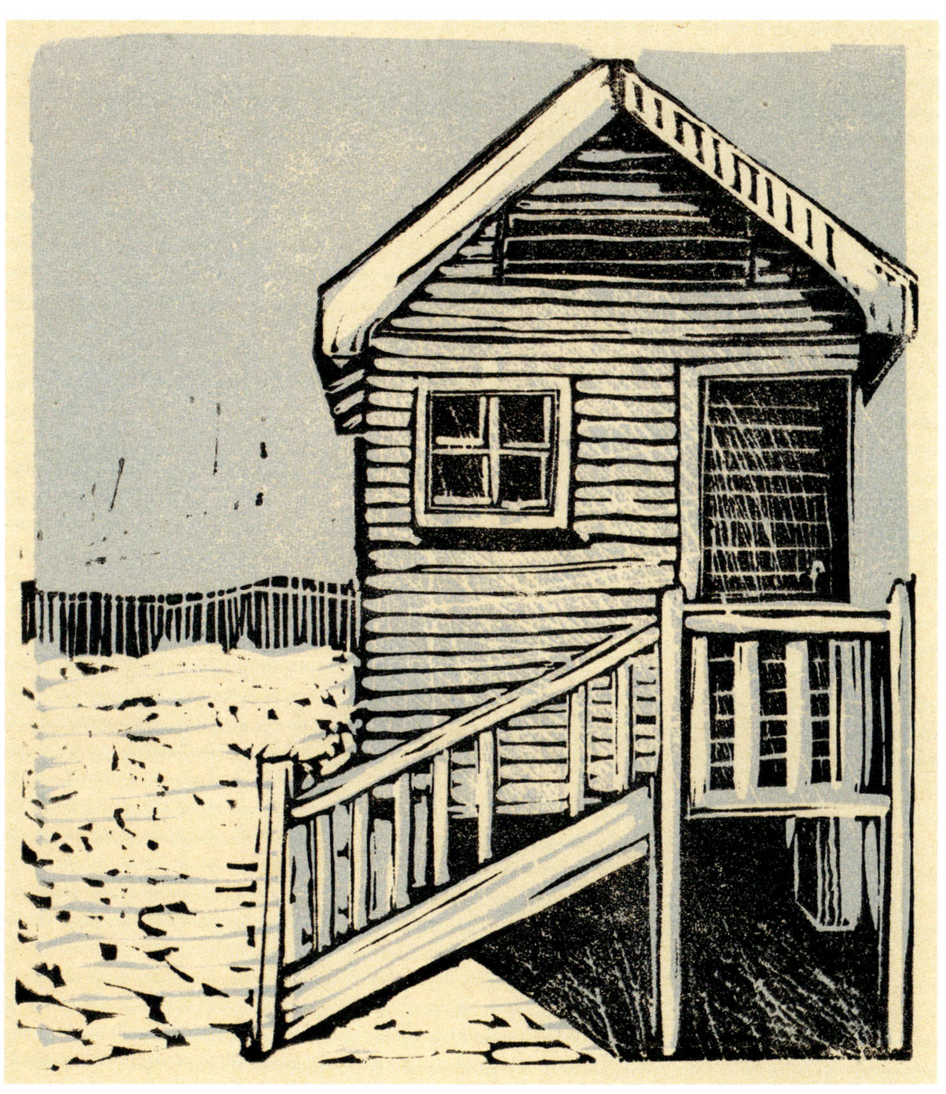

S.22.1 | colour reduction linocut
image: 16.8 x 15.2 cm | sheet: 35.5 x 23 cm | paper: newsprint
edition: unique impression
1st state: one line running through background wooden fence, printed in black and light blue

Muizenberg Beach–Bathing Hut*

WK : *The image of the bathing hut was the same thing. It would have been two blocks. You can see the registration is quite out—the light grey of the sky where it hits the black of the horizon and beach. These are beach huts on Muizenberg beach, but also at St James beach, that appear many years later in the film* Tide Table *[2003].*

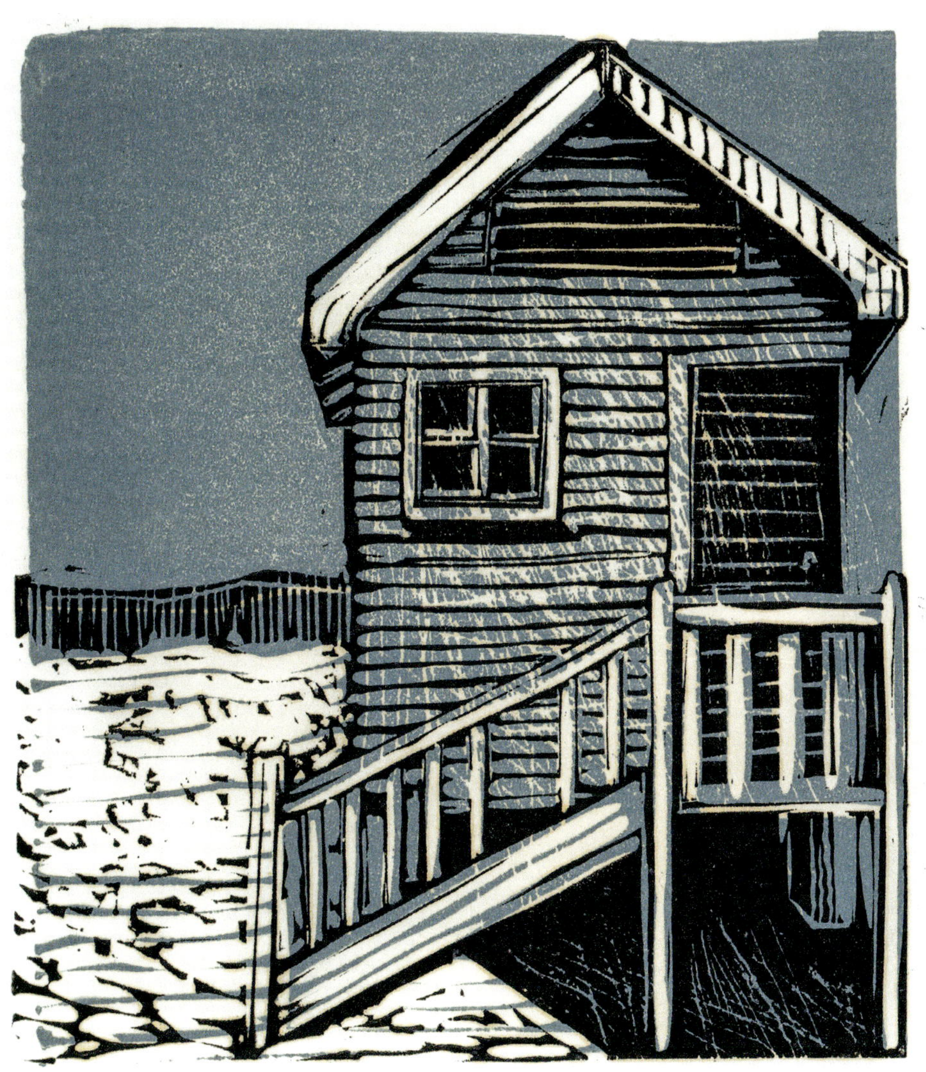

S.22.2 | colour reduction linocut
image: 16.8 x 15.2 cm | sheet: 31.8 x 23.8 cm | paper: mulberry paper
edition: not editioned, although at least 5 impressions printed; all impressions identified at time of publishing
printer/publisher: William Kentridge, Ainslie's Studios, Saxonwold, Johannesburg
signature style: WJK '77; some impressions unsigned
2nd and final state: two lines running through background wooden fence, printed in black and teal

Before

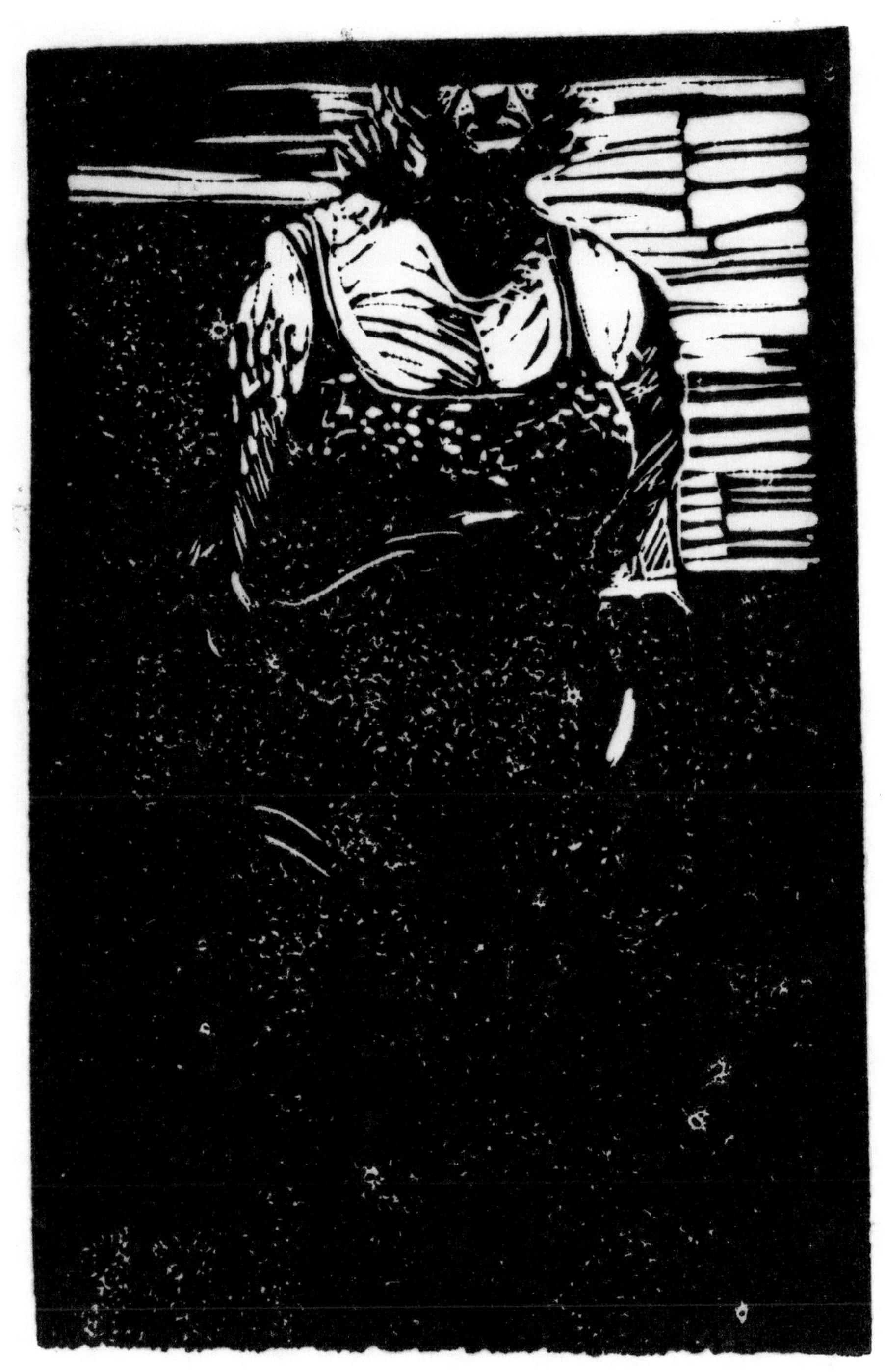

S.23.1 | linocut
image: 18.6 x 12.4 cm | sheet: 25.5 x 20.3 cm | paper: mulberry paper
edition: not editioned, although at least 3 impressions printed; 1 impression identified at time of publishing
1st state: woman in a one-piece swimming costume, without text

Before

WK : *This image would have been referenced from* Scope *magazine, or a similar magazine, in which there would have been two photographs: one 'before' [photograph] of a large lady, and the 'after', when some slimming programme had been followed and a lot of weight shed. I was always sympathetic with the 'before' images. The thing I never solved was how to do the hands—how to get the sense of the weight of the hand—and how to cut them into the block as they appear in the final state.*

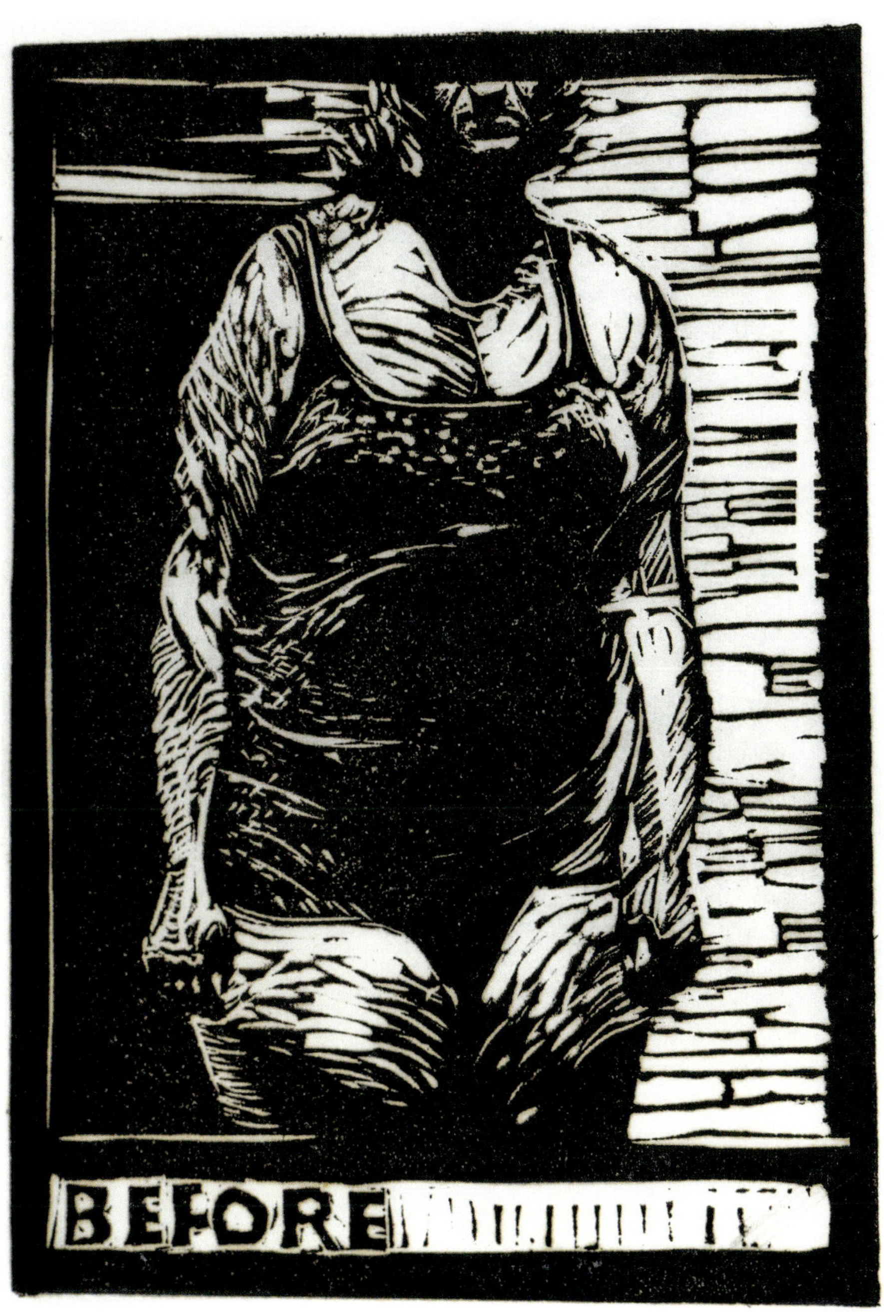

S.23.2 | reduction linocut
image: 17.5 x 12.4 cm | sheet: 23.5 x 16 cm | paper: mulberry paper
edition: 25 impressions; 5 impressions identified at time of publishing
printer/publisher: William Kentridge, Ainslie's Studios, Saxonwold, Johannesburg
signature style: WJK '77; KENTRIDGE, c. 2015; WJKentridge, December 2021; some impressions unsigned
2nd and final state: woman in a one-piece swimming costume, with text

Bare-Chested Man with Bathing Huts*

WK : *This image was again based on sketches done at Muizenberg, with the same beach huts behind the man with a 'Chai', the Hebrew symbol for life, worn on a gold chain around his neck. Muizenberg had traditionally been the holiday resort of Cape Town and, to an extent, Johannesburg Jewish communities. This is where my father and grandparents went on holiday, although by the sixties, when I went on holiday with my parents, it was to Plettenberg Bay further up the coast. On this linoleum block I tried scraping into the block using a burin, almost a drypoint in linoleum, seen best under the man's breast and in the hut behind him on the top right.*

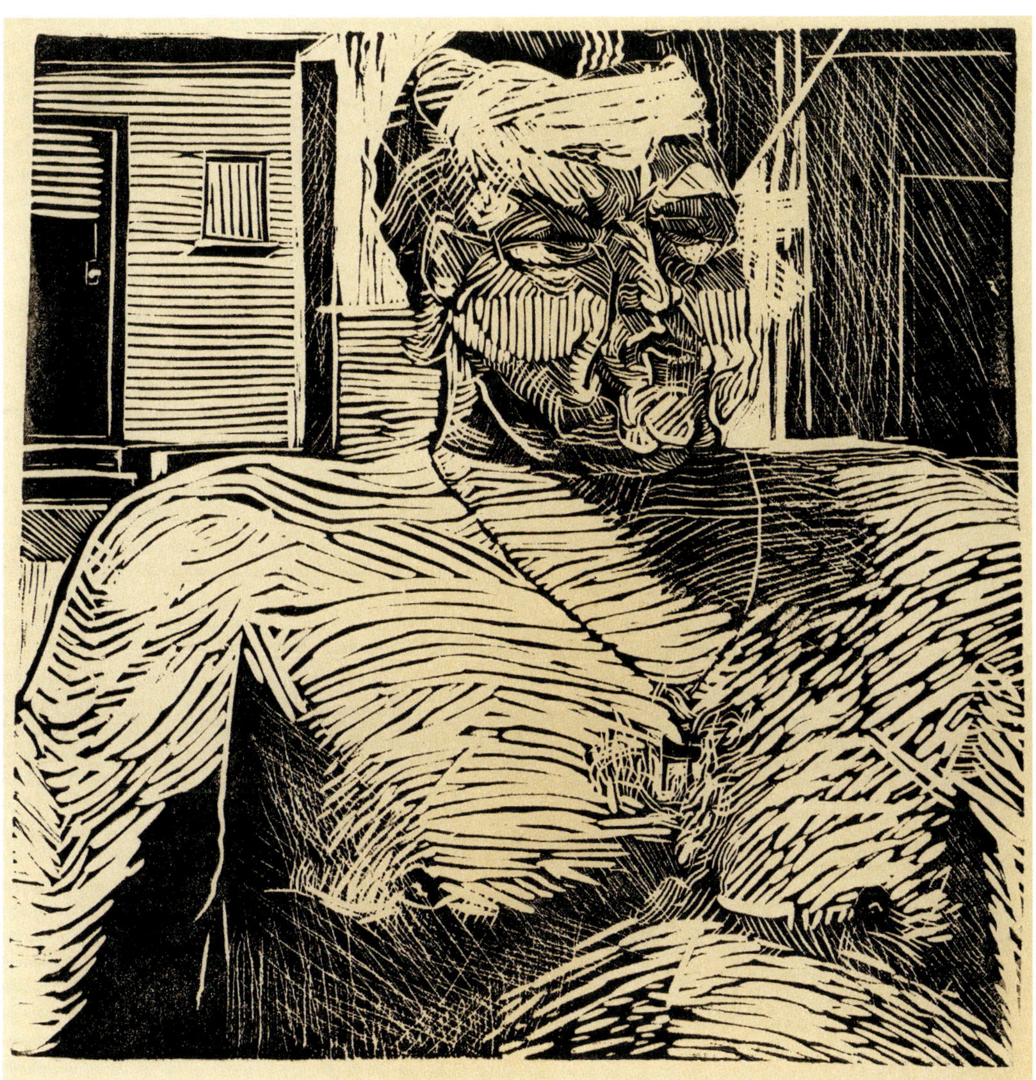

S.24 | linocut
image: 30.7 x 31 cm | sheet: 46 x 35.6 cm | paper: newsprint
edition: not editioned, although at least 3 impressions printed; 2 impressions identified at time of publishing
printer/publisher: William Kentridge, Ainslie's Studios, Saxonwold, Johannesburg
signature style: WJKentridge, c. 2018; some impressions unsigned

Bare-Chested Man with Bathing Hut–Version 2*

WK : *Another version of the same image, which I think I abandoned with only one impression pulled. Here I was trying to work a lot more roughly and much more violently. It looks as if there was an ink drawing done on the block and then cut out around the drawing on the block. This is a technique that I returned to in later years. The print feels closer to what I would like to be doing now, even though none were printed and it was abandoned as a clear failure.*

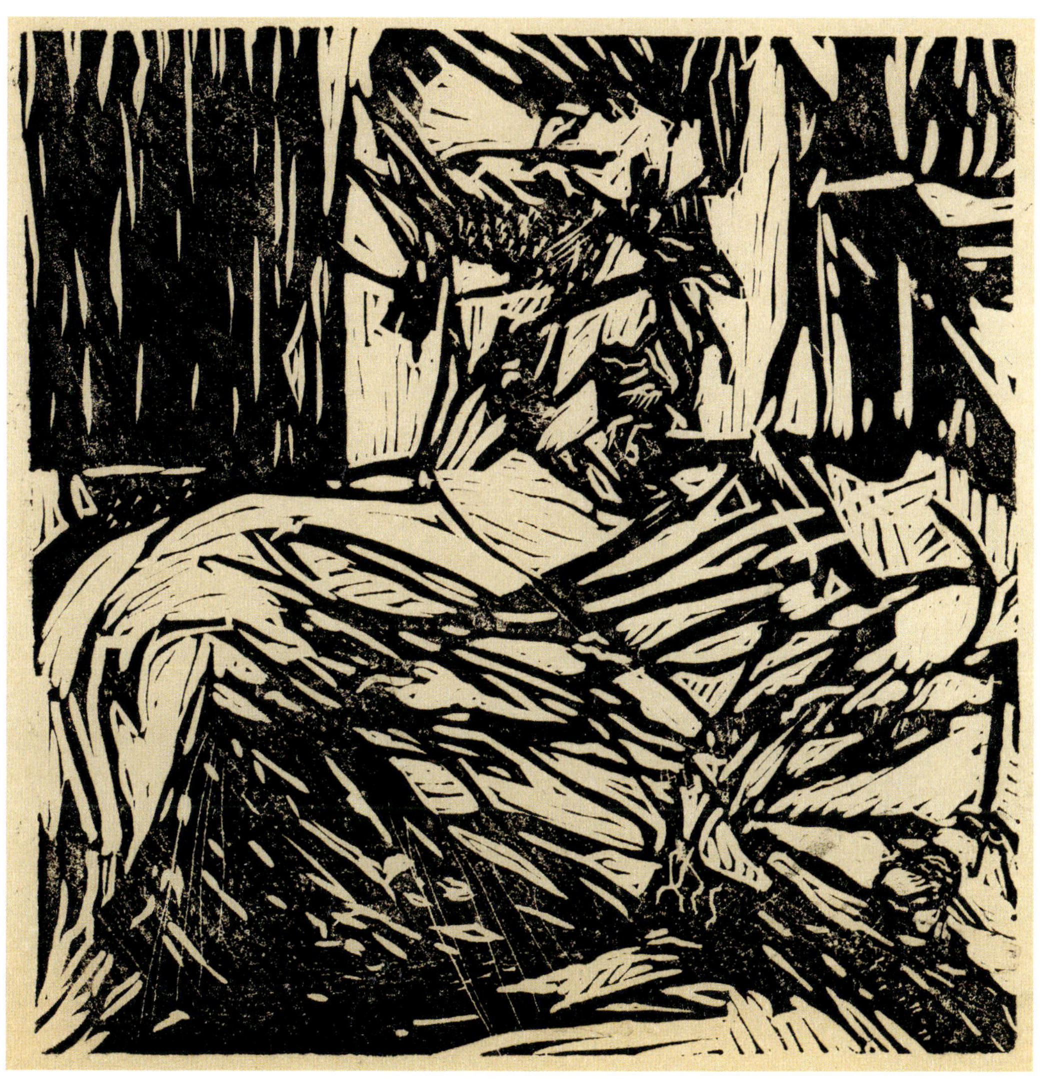

S.25 | linocut
image: 34.4 x 31 cm | sheet: 35.5 x 46 cm | paper: newsprint
edition: not editioned, although at least 3 impressions printed; 1 impression identified at time of publishing
printer/publisher: William Kentridge, Ainslie's Studios, Saxonwold, Johannesburg
signature style: unsigned

Chest and Chain, Muizenberg*

WK : *This is simply a detail, using a section of the block* Bare-Chested Man with Bathing Huts *[S. 24], using paper to block out the rolling up of the ink, perhaps the plate cut down. The colour variation would have been made using two blocks: the black plate, and then a second block with the pink and green on it.*

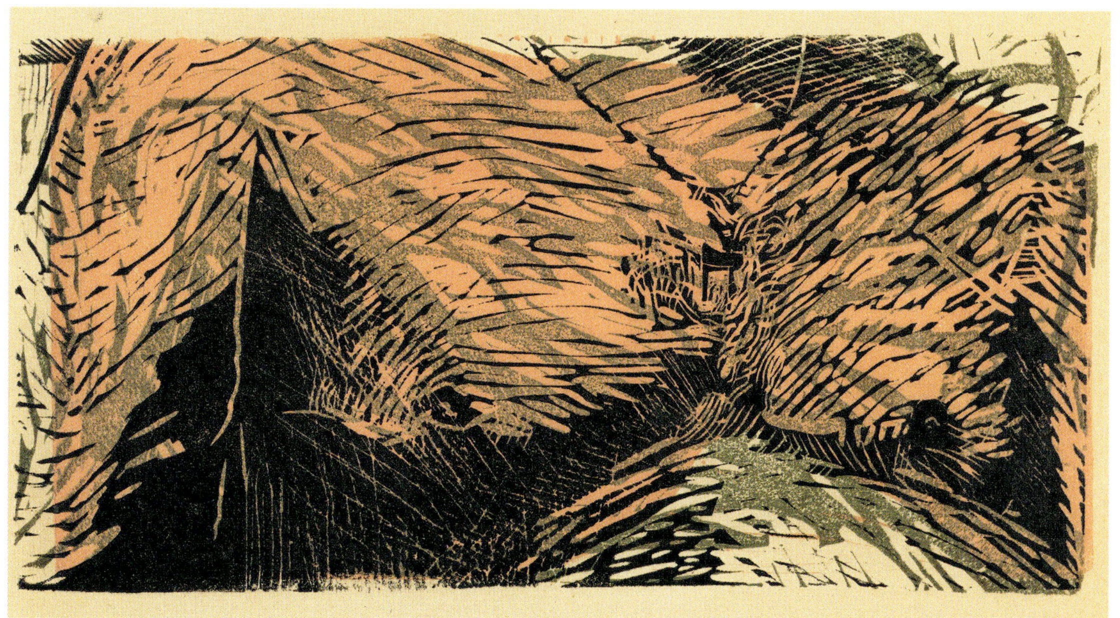

S.26.1 | colour linocut
image: 15.7 x 31.3 cm | sheet: 46 x 36.5 cm | paper: newsprint
edition: not editioned, although at least 3 impressions printed; 2 impressions identified at time of publishing
1st state: colour variation printed in black, pink and green

Chest and Chain, Muizenberg*

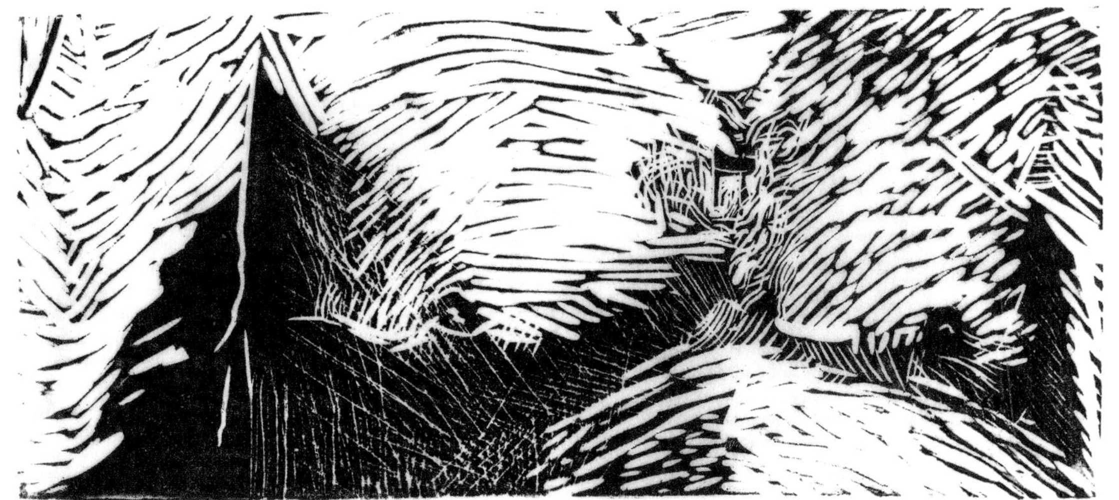

S.26.2 | linocut
image: 13.7 x 30.7 cm | sheet: 24 x 42 cm | paper: mulberry paper
edition: 25 impressions; 3 impressions identified at time of publishing
printer/publisher: William Kentridge, Ainslie's Studios, Saxonwold, Johannesburg
signature style: WJKentridge '77; some impressions unsigned
2nd and final state: printed in black with reduced height on the plate and added detail to right arm

THE MAKING OF THE *MUIZENBERG* PRINTS: TIMOTHY JAMES AND WILLIAM KENTRIDGE

* telephone conversation, 22 April 2025

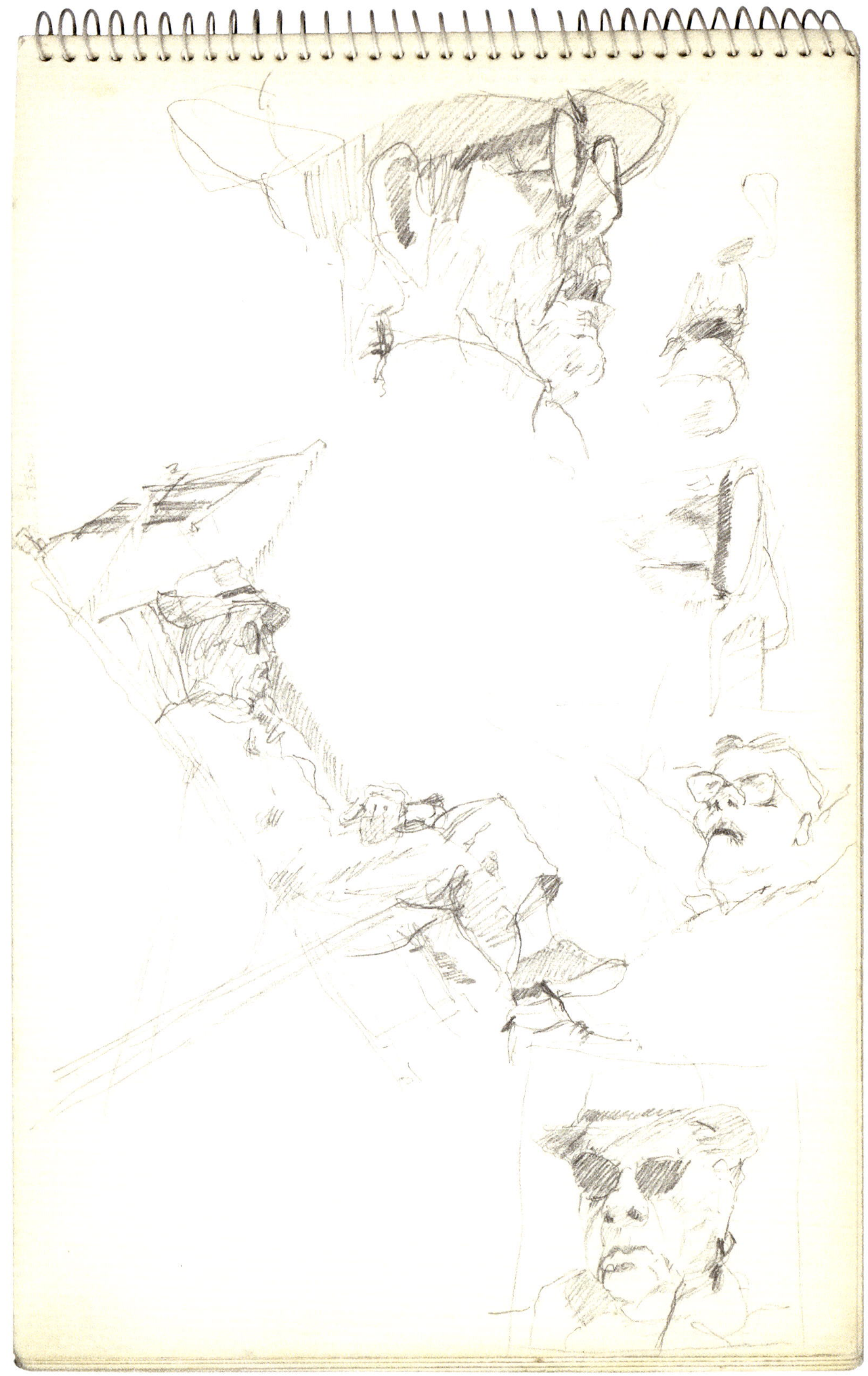

Fig. 1: Spiral-bound *Muizenberg* sketchbook, 1977. Pencil on Canson paper, 27 x 18 cm

Timothy James: Warren Siebrits and his team have been combing through your archives since 2019, putting together the puzzle that is your early print and poster output and, in the process, uncovering lost gems, such as the three early sketchbooks that include preparatory sketches for both the *Carlton Centre Games Arcade* and *Muizenberg* prints. One thing that occurred to me when looking at your *Muizenberg* prints, and the *Carlton Centre Games Arcade* etchings, is how naturalistic they are when compared to the slightly later *Domestic Scenes* series, with their Baconian space frames and deliberately unrealistic elements. What's noticeable in the Muizenberg material is how close some of the finished prints are to the sketchbook drawings.

William Kentridge: The drawings were done as sketches. I would go onto the beach in Muizenberg and sit with a small sketchbook and mainly draw people from behind or the side, because I didn't want to be seen staring at them. Muizenberg held different associations for me. It was not my family's holiday destination; it was the holiday destination of my parents' generation.

WK: Not personal family nostalgia, no—more for the Art Deco buildings.
There was this sense of the past in those bathing huts, which were certainly
there in our era, but are also very present in photographs from the thirties.
Many of the sketches were, as you say, quite naturalist, drawn from life, like
the large man in a bathing costume or the individual in a deckchair with their
hat over their face. So the sketches for both the *Muizenberg* and the *Carlton
Centre Games Arcade* series were very close to the prints. I worked from the
sketch straight onto the linoleum or the etching plate. I was also very drawn
to the largeness of some of the women as objects of desire.

TJ: Yes, because they do look forward to the prints of voluptuous women made a little
later in negligées rather than in swimming costumes (Siebrits 71-74). You did seem
to have this fascination with generously proportioned women despite the elegant
slimness of both your mother and your wife (girlfriend at the time). It's interesting.

WK: Yes, the muchness of flesh was fascinating to me at the time. Some images
were perhaps more satirical. Some of the negligée ones referenced pictures
from *Scope* magazine—you remember, the prurient magazine, with women
as naked as they were allowed to be in the seventies in South Africa. But there
would also be advertisements in the magazine for weight loss, with "before
and after" photographs. One of the linocuts from the Muizenberg period titled
Before (S.23) references those ads. It is interesting that that is one of the first
images I did with text in it, apart from the posters.

One of the things that came out of those Muizenberg sketches is an
image from the prints, where it exists as both a drawing and a linocut,
more particularly as a section of a linocut. The torso of a man (S.24-26) is
also the figure that is in one of the first etchings I did when I learned etching
with Giuseppe Cattaneo. It's the same man on a beach in *Already Dead
Awaiting Stuffing* (S.16). A nice drawing of the man, but there's a very badly
drawn hand on the woman, lower right. That was done with a colour roller,
a viscosity roller, on the etching plate.

TJ: With the *Muizenberg* prints, there's clearly a development in the passage between the drawings, which are quite nice, lively, naturalistic little drawings, and the much more considered compositions and effects in the prints. But you were still keeping the final images fairly simple, weren't you? *Already Dead Awaiting Stuffing* is one that is rather more complex in composition (even if, if I may say so, not all that successfully so).

WK: Yes. That one is an etching, but most of the *Muizenberg* prints are linocuts, and so are of necessity more simplified.

TJ: As you mentioned, *Already Dead Awaiting Stuffing* has colour in it. But you were also starting to play a little with colour in the linocuts. That was clearly a very experimental period for you.

WK: Yes, *Already Dead Awaiting Stuffing* was the second etching I had ever made and the first time I had ever used colour roll-ups. As for colour in the other *Muizenberg* prints, there are different ways of doing colour in linocuts. The one method is to have a different block for each colour—like Japanese woodcuts. Or you can do what is called reduction printing, for example the man in the deck chair (S.17), which has three colours—the white of the paper, the blue-grey mid-tone and black. It is a process of cutting away at the same block when adding different tones. It is an extremely considered way of making a print— the opposite way of making a print compared to an etching, and very much the opposite of a drawing.

TJ: Yes, it is very considered, isn't it? A very carefully calculated and executed process.

WK: You cut away one thing too many and that's it, it's done!

TJ: So you were working mostly from sketches at this time. There was that famous first *Muizenberg* print–*Muizenberg 1933* (S.10)–that was based on an old family photograph. (Incidentally, that's of course yet another example of text being already included in your work.)

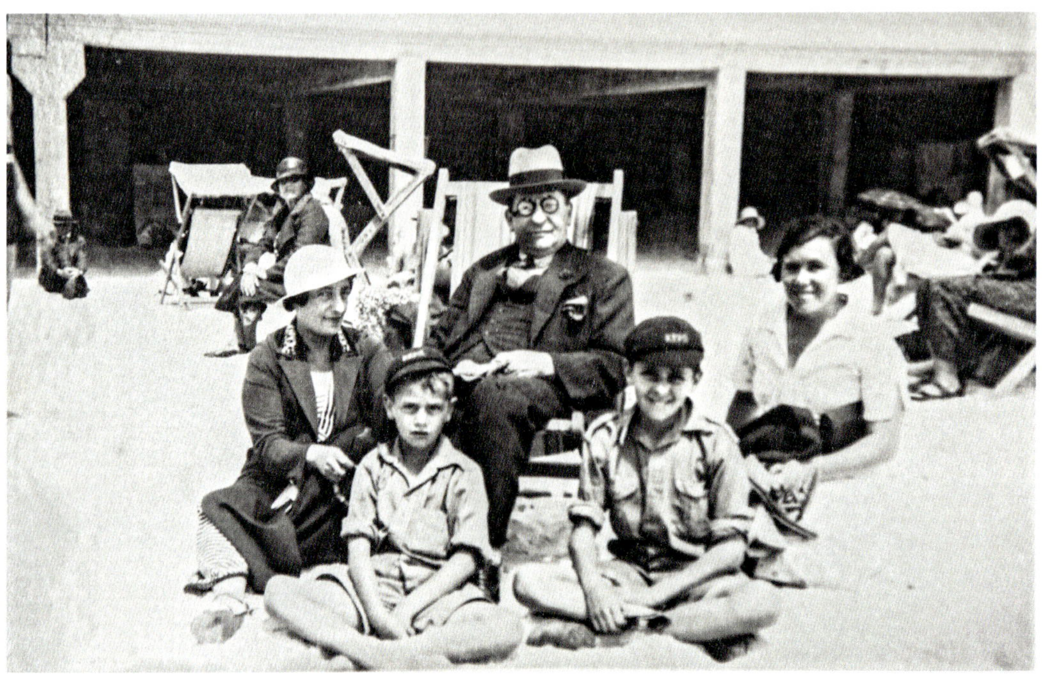

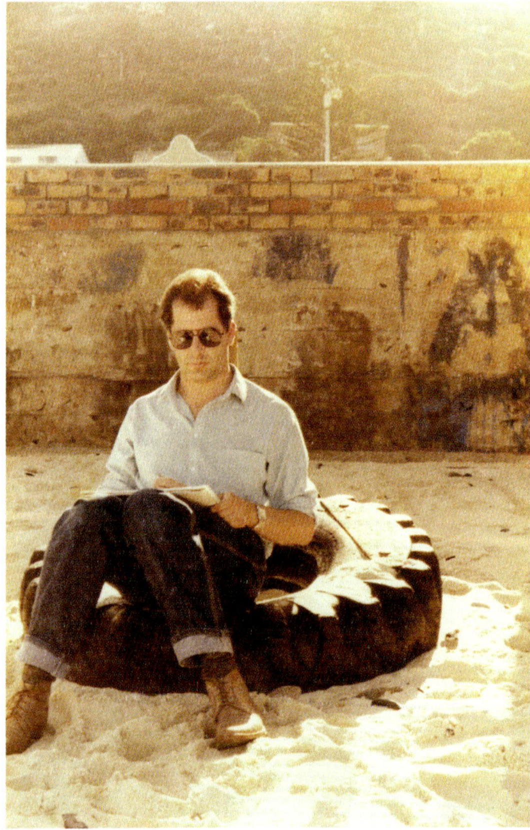

Fig. 2: Morris and May Kentridge, their sons Arnold and Sydney, with childminder, Edith Boon on Muizenberg beach, Cape Town, 1934.

Fig. 3: William Kentridge on Danger Beach, St. James, Cape Town, 1986. Photograph Timothy James

WK: Yes, that predated the others. I think it's on the basis of that linocut that the other *Muizenberg* prints came. We can date it because there was another linocut made at the same time based on a photograph. It was a group photo of Rhodes and company in Matabeleland, which was used on the cover of a university essay—so that would have been in 1976.

TJ: But then a bit later you started referencing material other than your own drawings, like the *Scope* magazine mentioned before. And so you actually moved away from some of those elements of what was, in a sense, social realism?

WK: Yes, in retrospect I regret that I didn't have 20 more sketchbooks with other scenes of life, as one does always have regret for such things.

TJ: One other thing that occurred to me, looking at the first three series that are coming out in these more manageable little books–this one after the *Domestic Scenes* and the *Carlton Centre Games Arcade* series … I really love those games-of-chance etchings, by the way, with that wonderful Goyaesque aquatint and the brooding figures.

WK: Yes, so do I! Somehow the hunched bodies, the closeness, the rough jackets all translated well from those sketches into the prints. There are always regrets—I look back at those early works and think there are such interesting elements to them and I wonder why I stopped there. But at the time that you're making the work, there is such anxiety and you are wondering, 'Oh my God! Is this what art should be? This looks so old-fashioned!'

TJ: So, to return to the three groups of etchings that these books have closely looked at so far, you did quite a lot of these more focused series or groups. You'd go to the amusement arcades in Johannesburg centre, and you'd have that as a subject. Then a trip to Muizenberg produced a number of pictures from there. Then the *Domestic Scenes* was clearly linked in general subject matter, partly theoretically, I suppose.

Perhaps after that there was a sort of expansion of focus. I remember in the eighties, for example, on your visit to me in Cape Town, when I took that photo of you on Danger Beach, sitting on the car tyre, sketching. That suggests a rather different way of seeking images and ideas to transmute into art. What we did that day, as I remember, was drive down the peninsula along the coast and inland over the Ou Kaapse Weg past the Silvermine Nature Reserve. And we would stop at regular distances—I would take a photograph of something and you would make a sketch of whatever happened to be there.

WK: I remember we would purposefully travel irregular distances. We would get in the car and choose an arbitrary distance, say 8.3 kilometres. We would drive exactly 8.3 kilometres and then we'd stop and get out.

TJ: Oh, yes. I remember doing the same thing with you up in the Highveld, also sometime in the mid-eighties. We would drive out of Johannesburg and stop after a certain random, arbitrary distance. Again, the whole point was to avoid choosing an interesting or attractive subject and for you to rather just draw what was there.

WK: It was a way of trying to avoid the picturesque and not saying, 'Let's drive until we find a nice view.' Rather drive a certain distance and see what is there and find a different way of looking at a landscape. And the ones that work are really a non-landscape. But, of course, the habits of the eye are strong and it's hard to stop having the shadow in the foreground and the leaf coming in from the side and so on.

TJ: So when did you decide that this unorthodox approach was a good idea? Because, in a sense, the *Muizenberg* prints are more traditional in composition and quite picturesque, aren't they?

WK: Yes, they are more traditional in a sense. I can't remember exactly how this driving/drawing exercise was conceptualised, But there is a nice drawing that was in my parents' house in London of you crouching down at a gate, taking a photograph at the edge of a ditch or a culvert, which was, again, to get kind of the most non-landscape one could find.

TJ: Pity I never possessed quite the same potential as a photographer that you had as a draughtsman.

WK: I did the same sort of thing but with small etchings when I was in Tuscany in 1996. I would walk, say, one hundred and fifty paces and draw what was to the left or the right of me. There I'd do it in the form of a Claude glass, where I'd polish an etching plate very very brightly and, after that certain number of paces, I'd hold the plate up in front of me like a mirror and try to draw what was reflected directly onto the polished surface. But you need a steady hand, or a stand to put the plate on. There are so many things to do like that with an etching plate—that kind of spontaneous drawing.

TJ: Another instance of a similar thing, perhaps: I remember around this time that, after I'd come to have supper with you and Anne, you and I would settle down and do little watercolours of more-or-less arbitrary small objects. I still have one that you made of a few objects I'd left behind. You dated it for my birthday in 1977. So it has, in fact, been a persistent sort of modus operandi for a long time.

WK: Yes, exactly—though I haven't done it so much recently.

TJ: We've moved from Muizenberg in 1978 as far as Tuscany in 1996 and again in 1999. Let's go back there. Firstly, you spoke of turning your sketch of me crouching in a non landscape into a full-sized drawing. But the *Muizenberg* sketches—and the Carlton Centre ones, for that matter—were turned into modestly sized prints. Why didn't you work any sketches into larger drawings back then, as you were to start doing to such effect just a few years later?

WK: Because the Muizenberg drawings and prints were made before I had found working with charcoal drawings as my main medium. At that stage I

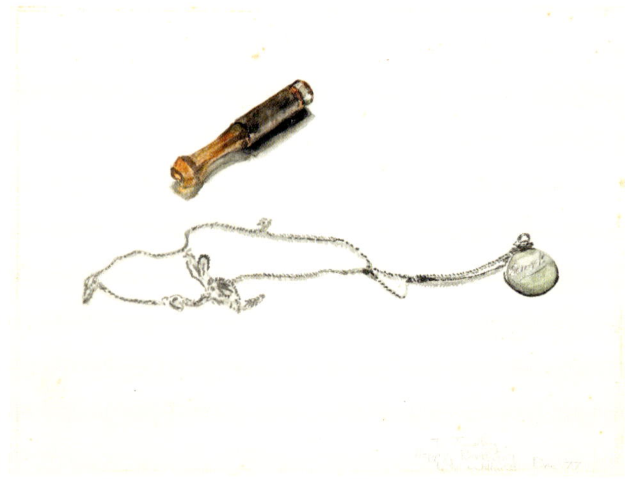

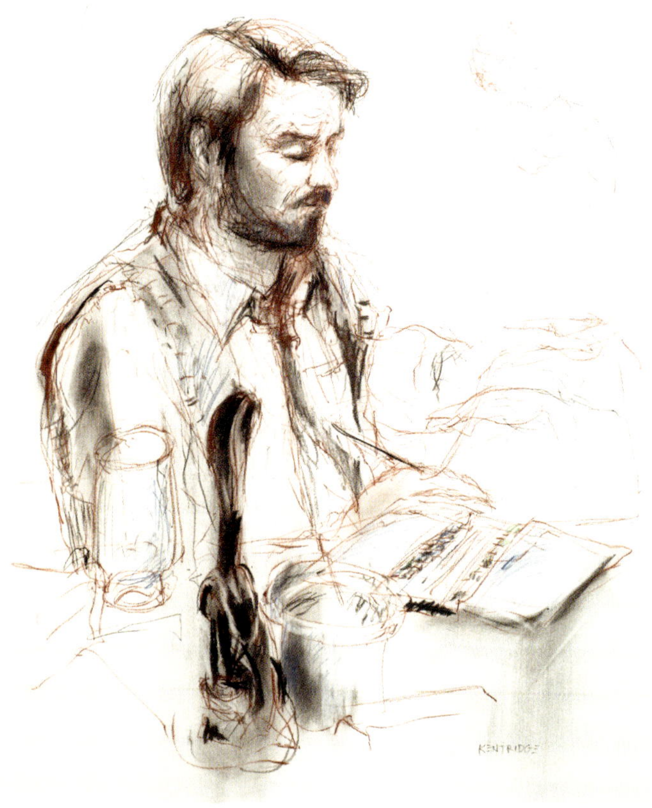

Fig. 4: ***To Timothy | Happy Birthday | Love, William***, Dec 1977. Watercolour on Canson paper, 18.5 x 25 cm
Fig. 5: ***Timothy James***, 1986. Conté and charcoal on paper, 71.5 x 56.5 cm

was exclusively making prints. The drawings were done in pencil, and I was still thinking at that stage of painting in oil as the way I'd go for larger work. By the time I drew the landscape with you crouching down, I knew that they would not become paintings. They had no ambition to become paintings.

TJ: Looking at the *Muizenberg* prints, there are already a few of your later motifs apparent. I don't think there is a coffee pot in sight yet [William chuckles], but there are the fat women and the sunglasses that we see plenty more of in later years.

WK: And the striped suit! It's a suit in the case of my grandfather, which becomes the pinstriped swimming costumes of some of the men on the beach. And then the pinstriped suit of Soho Eckstein, who has retired to Muizenberg in the animated film *Tide Table* (2003).

TJ: Wow! This is all a long time ago that we're talking about, Will. We're getting old.

WK: Yes. Nearly fifty years to the first *Muizenberg* image. You think of all the people who did their great work before the age of thirty-five and you do feel old.

TJ: I remember a long while back sitting on a bus and seeing a mother praise something of her little boy's—a drawing or whatever—and thinking, a little sneeringly, that by that age Mozart had already written a dozen operas and symphonies. And then suddenly realising that by the time Mozart was my age (back then), he was already dead and I hadn't exactly achieved much by comparison!

WK: One thing that's striking when you think of the great writers and musicians who died young is the amount of work they must have done every day. I mean, the number of [musical] notes written by Schubert in those few years he had.

TJ: But don't you look back at yourself and think how much you did in those days when you were young, while you were busy with so many art-related things as well as university work?

WK: Well, I think now, 'My God! What was all this endless running? Why was I running so hard?' I believe it is partly our generation, for me partly familial and, of course, partly the pleasure of it … that excitement as the print comes through the press.

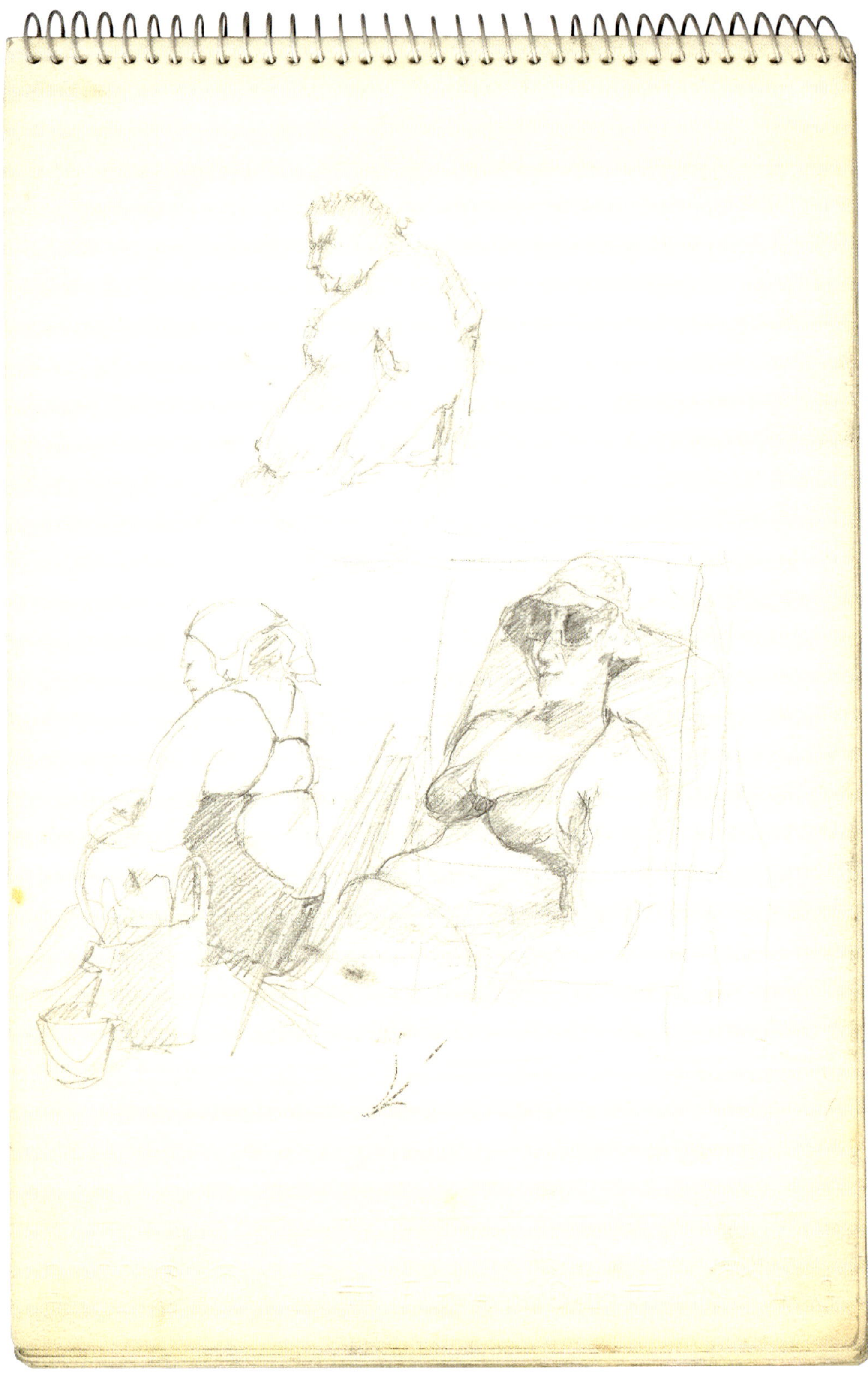

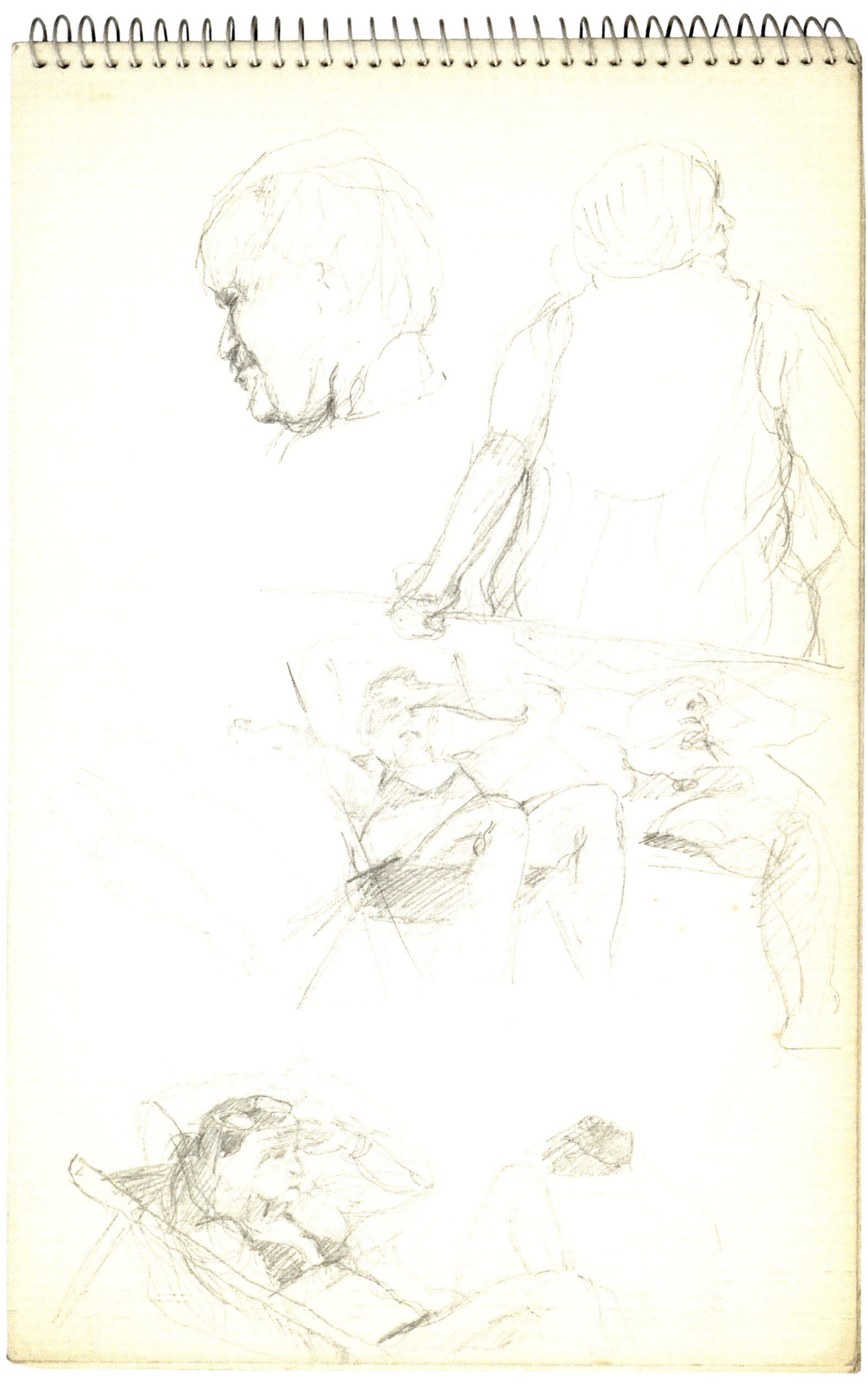

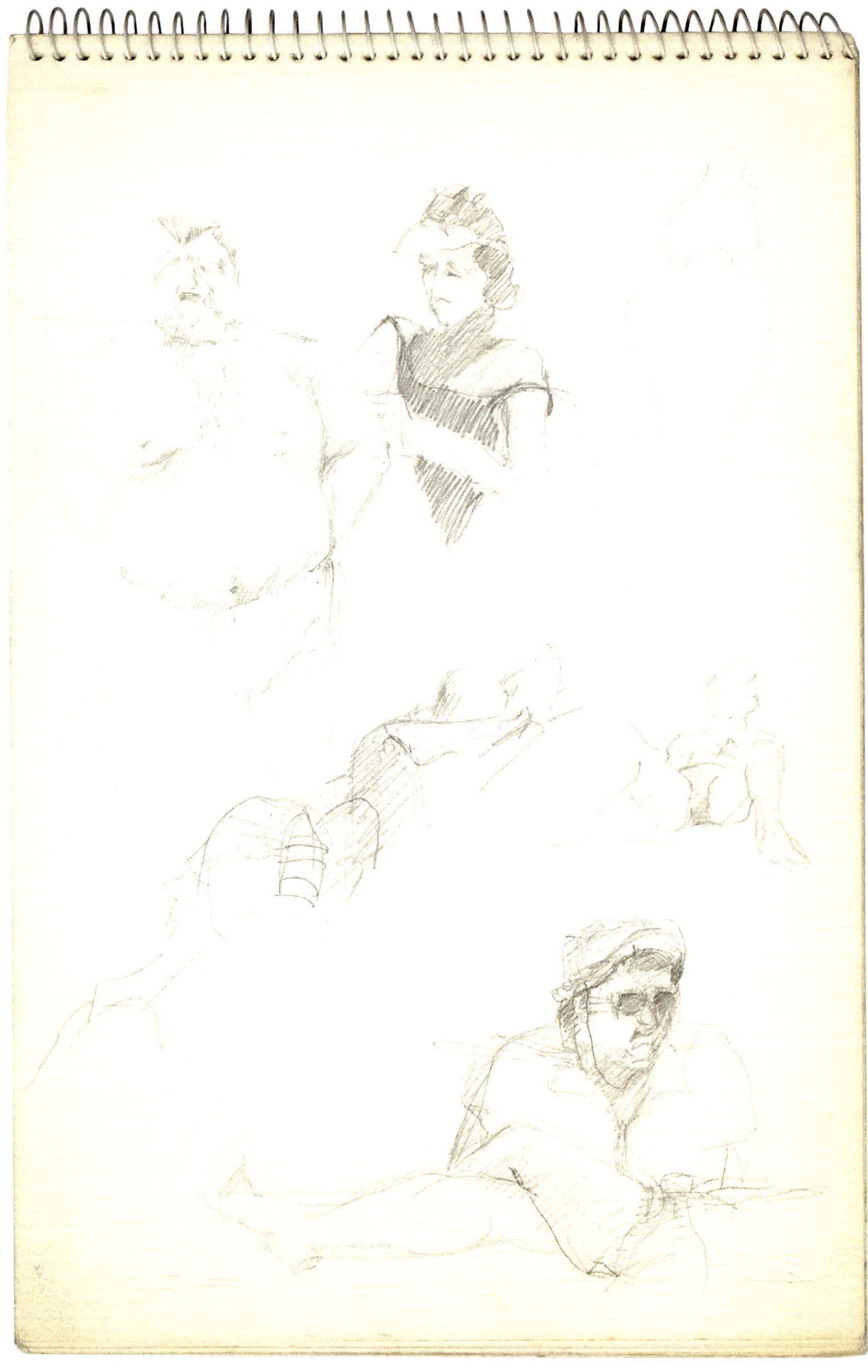

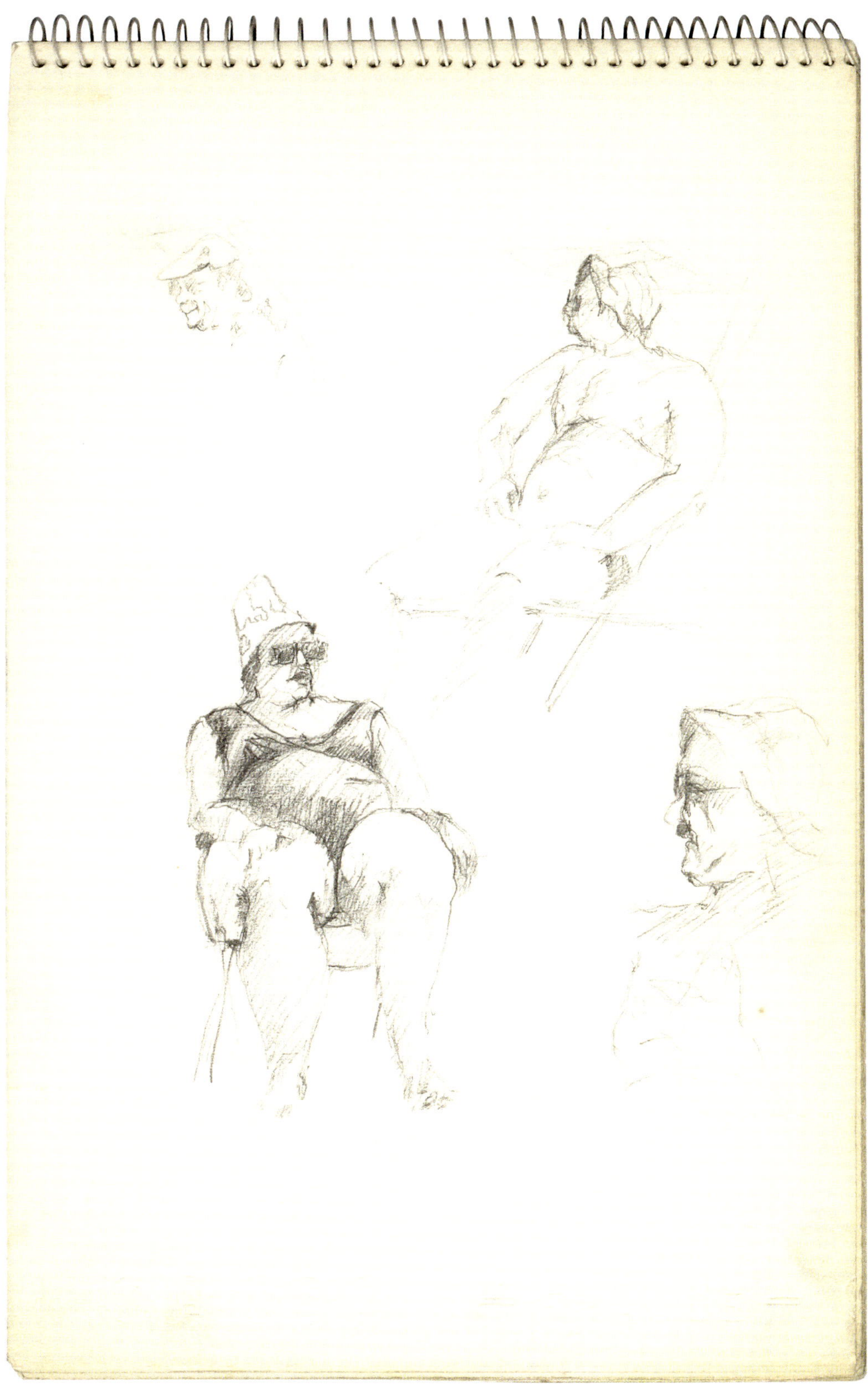

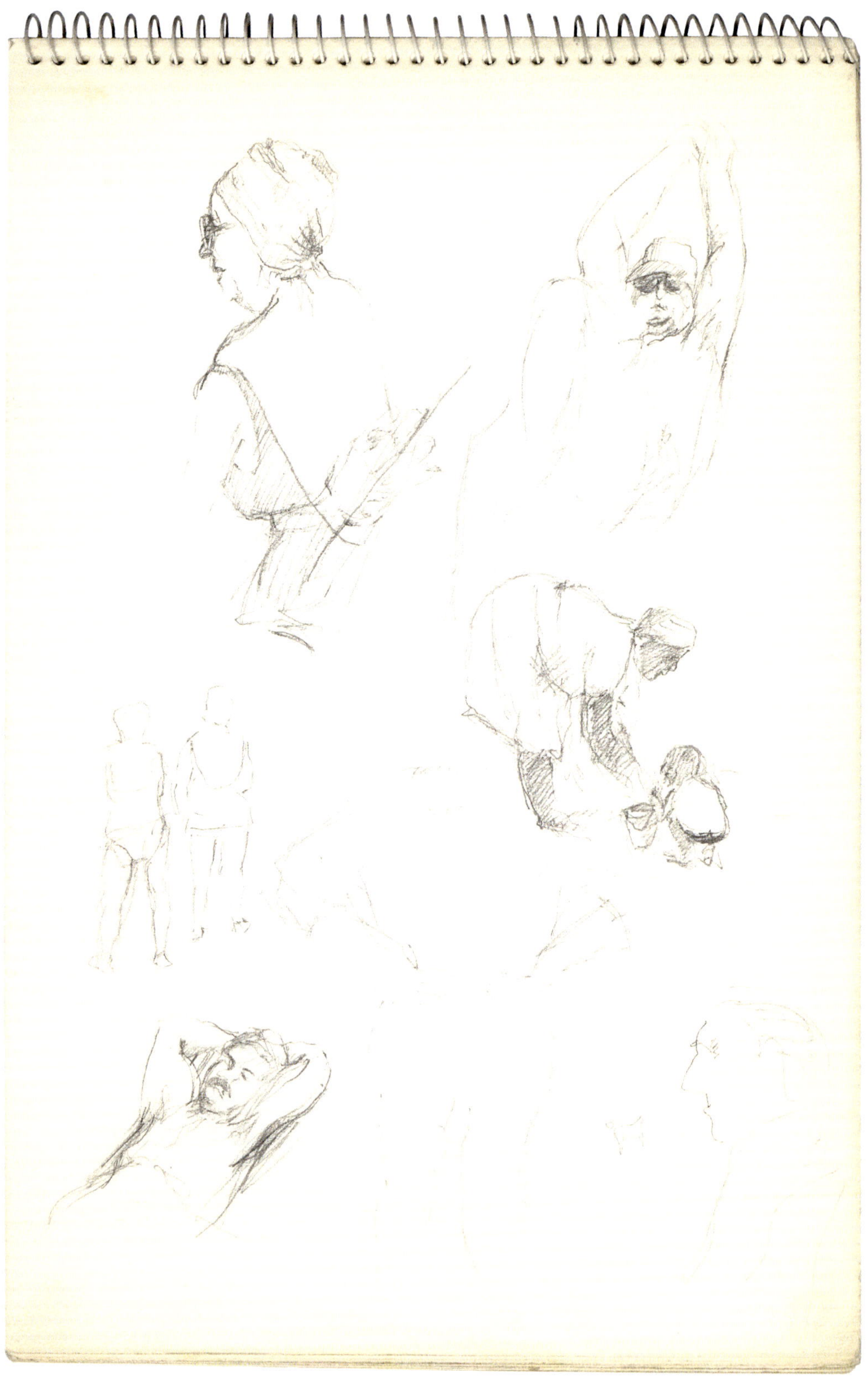

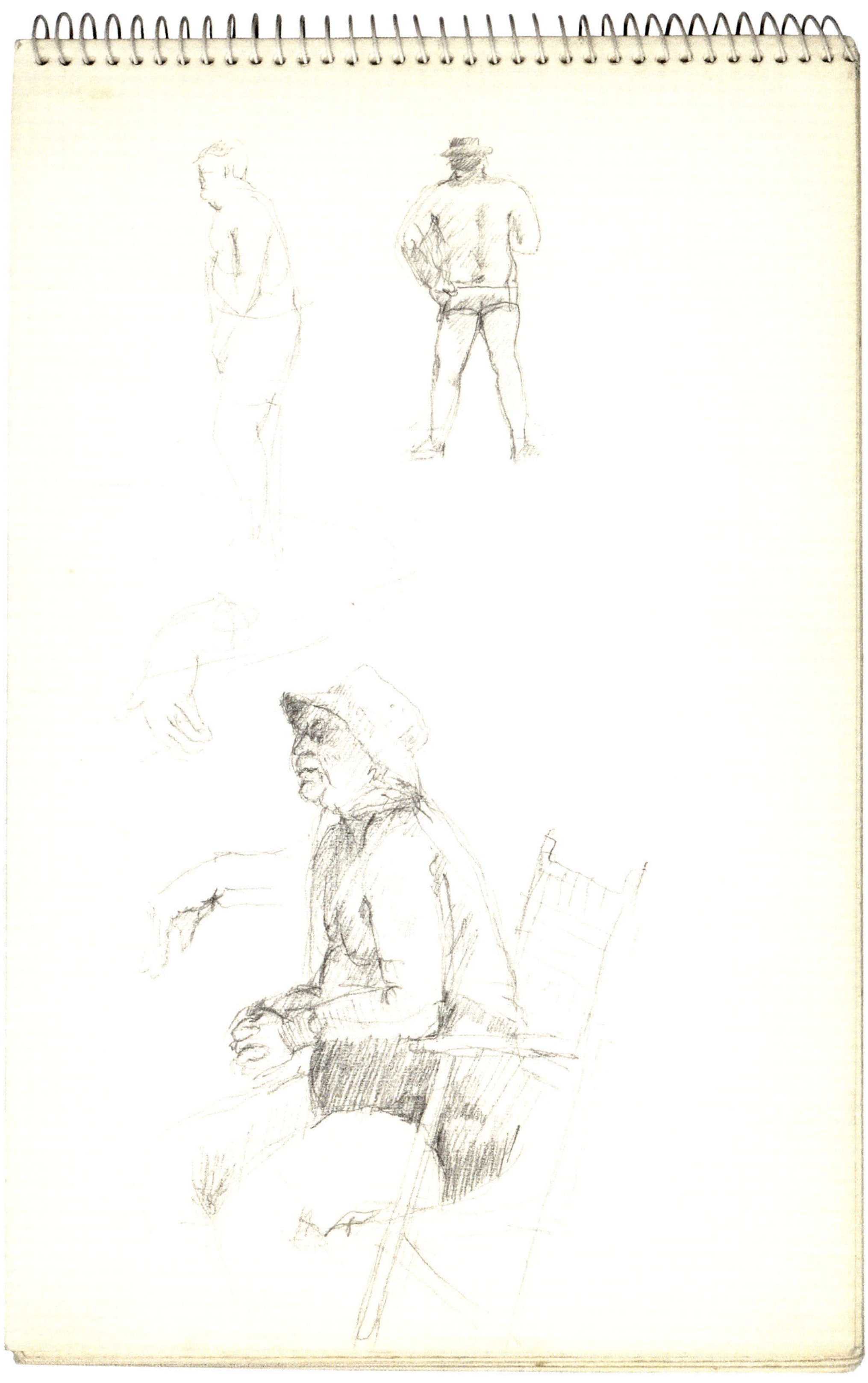

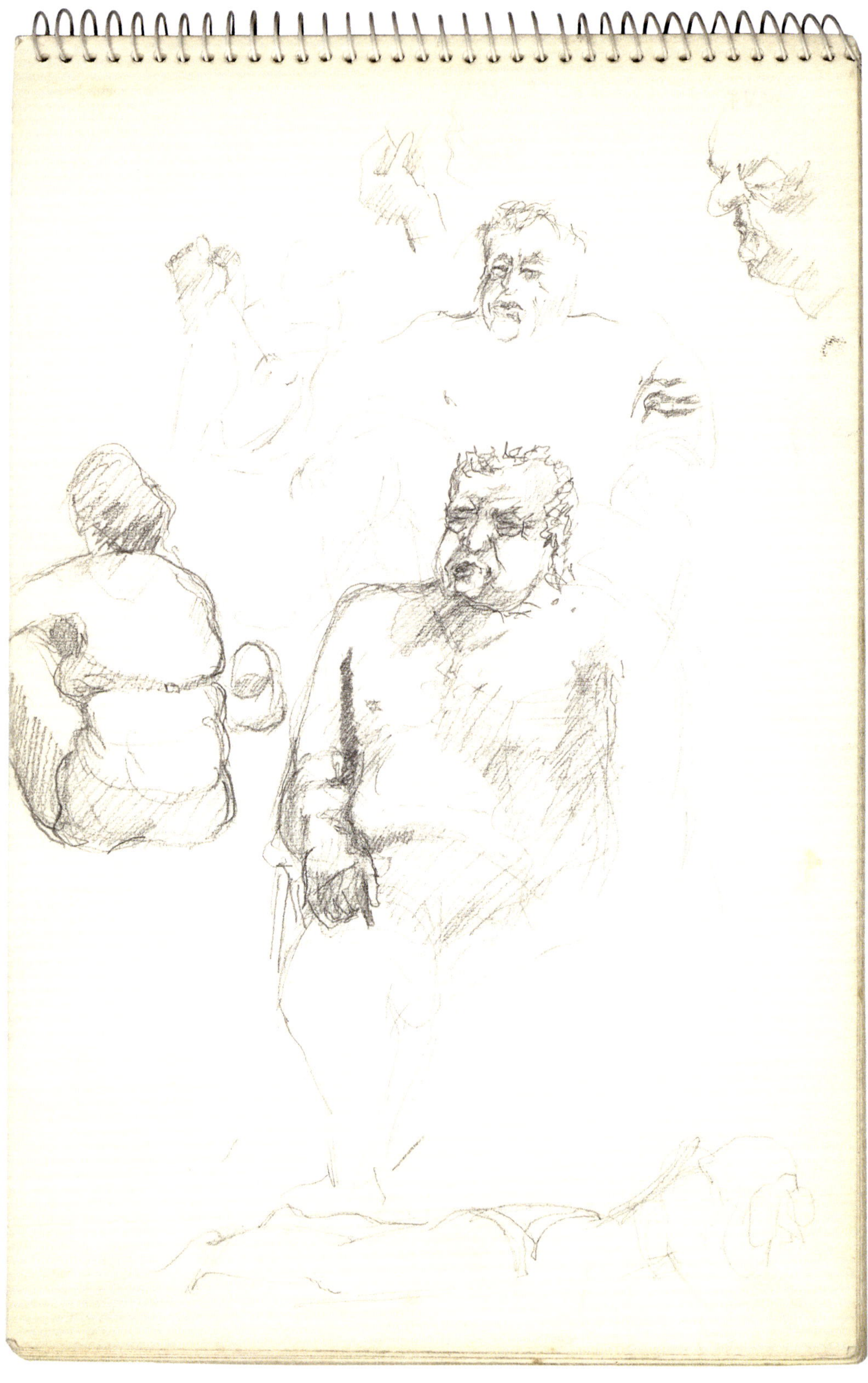

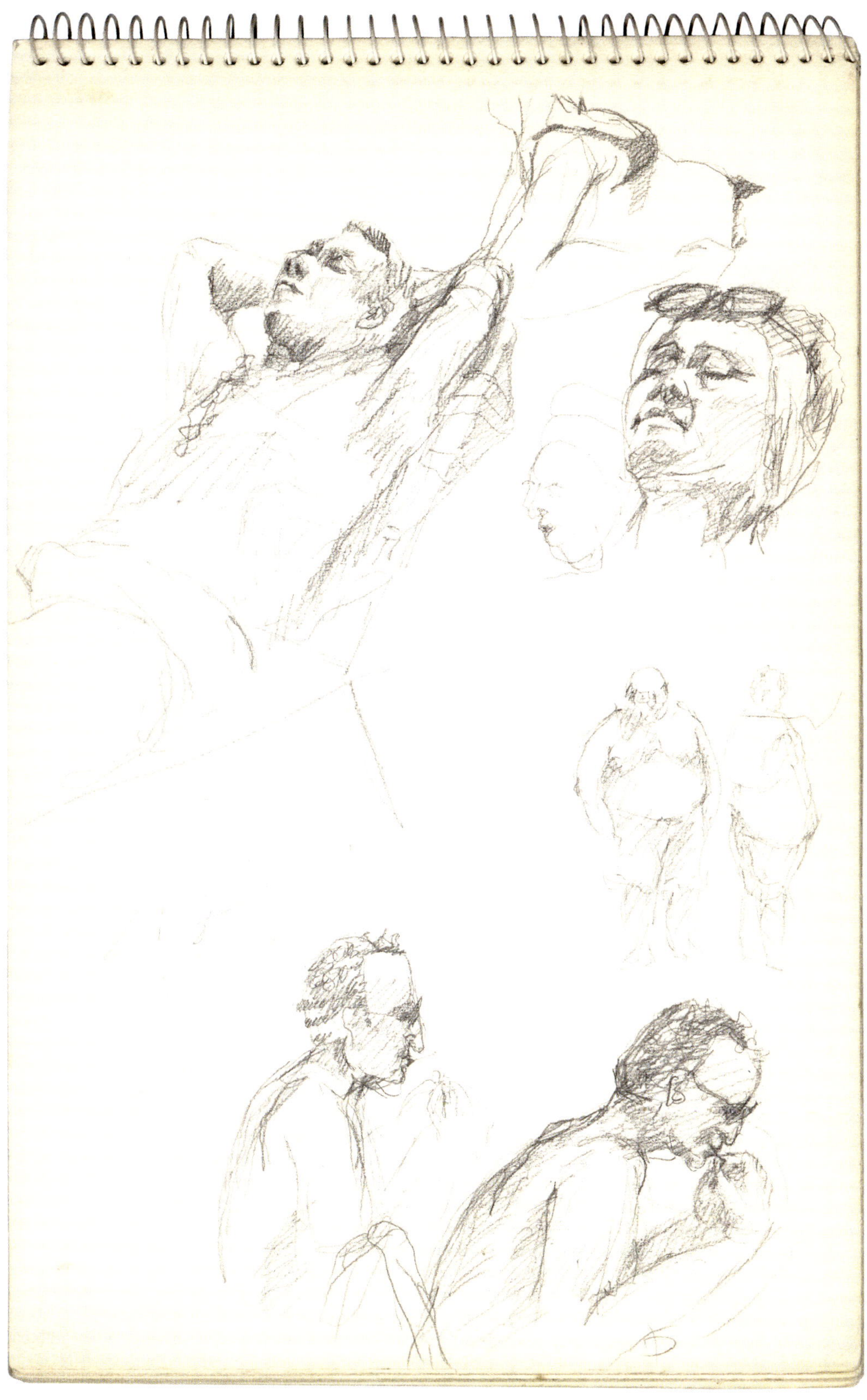

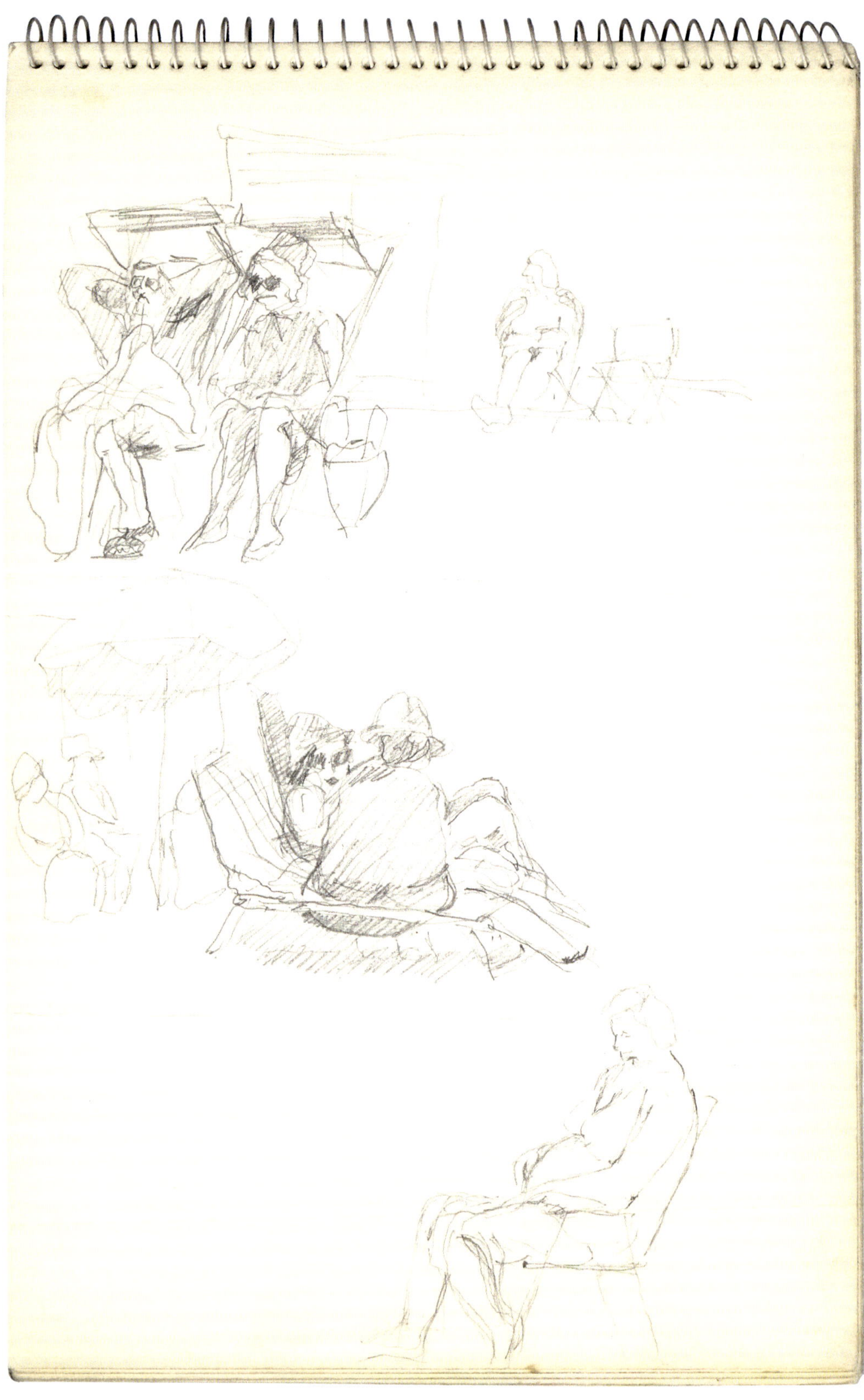

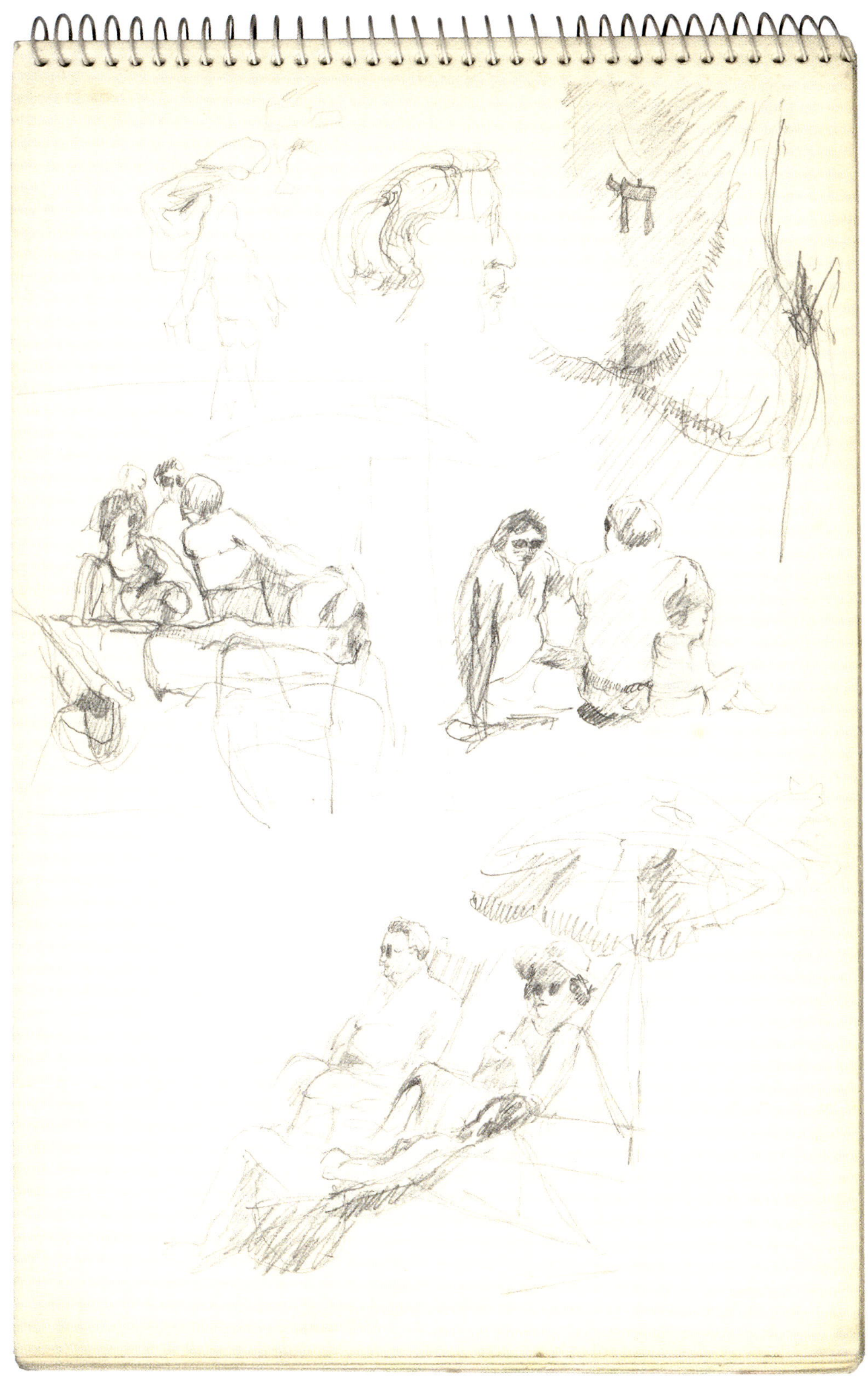

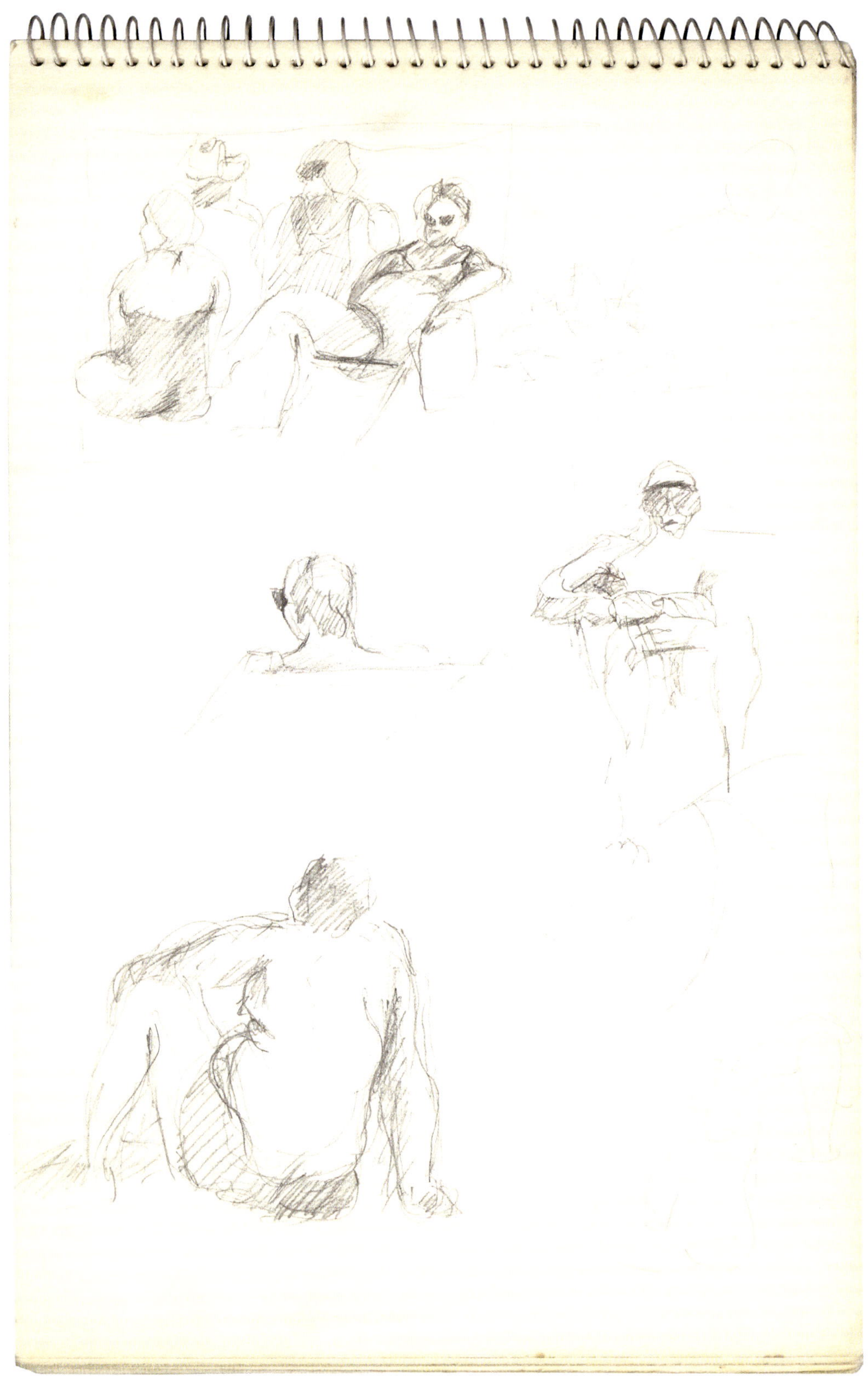

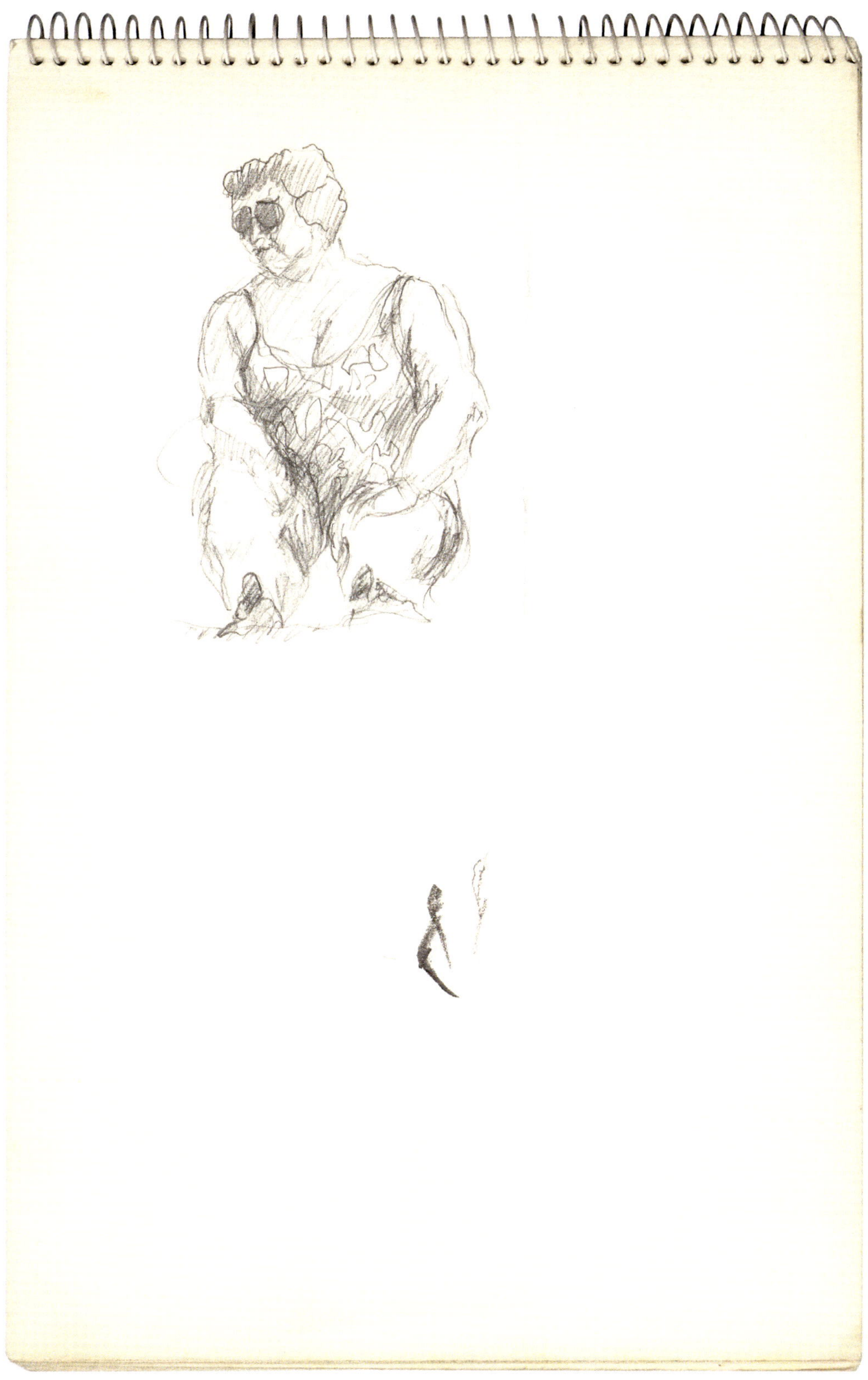

TITLES |

The majority of prints made during the period 1974–1979 were not publicly exhibited and therefore were never given formal titles by the artist at the time they were first printed. The correct historical titles have been identified and used in all cases where the work was commercially exhibited and original price lists or exhibition catalogues listing these titles could be traced. Any print that has a title, caption or slogan contained within the composition of the work itself has been titled in accordance with said information. Where information was unavailable, a brief descriptive title has been provided instead. These works are marked with an asterisk.

NUMBERING |

Each work has been catalogued numerically for this publication with a Siebrits number as S.16, S.17, S.18 etc., where S=Siebrits, and is listed chronologically. The Siebrits number is a chronological numbering system established to accurately catalogue all William Kentridge prints and posters reproduced in *William Kentridge Catalogue Raisonné Volume 1. Prints and Posters 1974–1990*. For this publication the decision was made to keep the Siebrits numbers consistent with those in the catalogue raisonné to facilitate cross referencing.

Where more than one impression of a work is documented, these are numbered progressively in relation to the original Siebrits number, as S.10.1, S.10.2, S.10.3 etc; where more than one state of a work is documented, these are numbered progressively in relation to the impression number, as S.10.7i, S.10.7ii etc.

SKETCHBOOK |

Spiral-bound ***Muizenberg*** sketchbook, 1977. Pencil on Canson paper, 27 x 18 cm.

This sketchbook, made during the summer holidays of 1977, was discovered at the Kentridge studio after a returned exhibition crate was opened by the studio staff in early 2025. All thirteen pages have been digitally scanned and reproduced, for the first time, in this volume.

LIST OF WORKS |

S.10	Muizenberg 1933 (7 states, 2 variations)
S.16	Already Dead Awaiting Stuffing (4 states)
S.17	Muizenberg Beach–Old Man Seated in Deckchair* (2 states)
S.18	Muizenberg Beach–Man Wearing Sunglasses and Beach Hat* (3 states)
S.19	Muizenberg Beach–Man with Sunglasses* (1 state)
S.20	Muizenberg Beach–Man with Arms Behind his Back* (5 states)
S.21	Muizenberg Beach–Woman on Towel with Sunglasses* (3 states, 1 variation)
S.22	Muizenberg Beach–Bathing Hut* (2 states)
S.23	Before (2 states)
S.24	Bare-Chested Man with Bathing Huts* (1 state)
S.25	Bare-Chested Man with Bathing Hut–Version 2* (1 state)
S.26	Chest and Chain, Muizenberg* (2 states)

TIMOTHY JAMES ON MEETING WARREN SIEBRITS |

When I needed to sell some of my Kentridge drawings and prints in the early 2000s, William recommended Warren to me as being deeply knowledgeable, interested in the artist's past, and sympathetic. Warren visited me in Cape Town one morning, and we spent the rest of the day and evening talking together and became good friends. I can still picture Warren sitting on my sofa as I hauled out the pictures–I had nearly forty back then–and I remember noticing that he was wearing Gucci shoes! I met Lunetta, Warren's partner and collaborator, soon after and the friendship widened. It was some years later, when I was clearing up stuff (I'm a chucker), that I gave Warren (a hoarder/collector) the postcards that I had received from William over the years, featuring art that he'd seen and liked in galleries, as well as the photo I'd taken of him on Danger Beach in the mid-eighties.

TIMOTHY JAMES ON TIM JAMES |

Tim was a student of History of Art at Wits University when he met and became friends with William–both of them were involved in the student movement, NUSAS [National Union of South African Students]. Later, while living in England for eight years, Tim was a witness at William's marriage to Anne in London. He went on to get a PhD in English, but never seemed to have a respectable job, though he has much enjoyed a professional involvement in wine, particularly writing about it. Tim has lived in Cape Town since 1986.

First edition published in 2025

Researcher and author: Warren Siebrits
Conversation: Timothy James
Book design: Lunetta Bartz
Text, image and cataloguing editor: Lucia Duncan
Additional editing: Elizabeth Sleith
Proofreader: Lynda Stephenson
Photography: Thys Dullaart and Mike Hall
Scanning: Frank Marshall at Silvertone, Johannesburg
Digital reproductions: Steidl image department
Separations: Steidl image department
Production and printing: Steidl, Göttingen

Steidl
Düstere Straße 4 / 37073 Göttingen, Germany
Phone +49 551 49 60 60
mail@steidl.de
steidl.de

ISBN 978-3-96999-244-9
Printed in Germany by Steidl